P9-DMM-760

SAP

SAP

An Executive's Comprehensive Guide

Grant Norris
Ian Wright
James R. Hurley
John Dunleavy
Alison Gibson

JOHN WILEY & SONS, INC.

New York • Chichester • Weinheim • Brisbane • Singapore • Toronto

Copyright © 1998 by Coopers & Lybrand L.L.P. All rights reserved.

Published by John Wiley & Sons, Inc.

Published simultaneously in Canada.

Library of Congress Cataloging-in-Publication Data:

SAP : an executive's comprehensive guide / Grant Norris . . . [et al.].
    p.   cm.
    Includes index.
    ISBN 0-471-24992-0 (cloth: alk. paper)
    1. SAP R/3.   2. Business—Computer programs.   3. Client/server
computing.   I. Norris, Grant.
  HF5548.4.R2S26 1998
  650'.0285'53769—dc21   97-51809

Printed in the United States of America.

10 9 8 7 6 5 4 3

About the Contributors

John Dunleavy, BA, MBA, ABD, CPA
Jack is a Senior Partner in Coopers & Lybrand's Telecommunications, Media, and Utilities group based in Parsippany, New Jersey. He is the co-author of *Reinventing the CFO—Moving from Financial Management to Strategic Management*. He has been involved in implementing SAP R/3 since 1995.

James R. Hurley, BA, MBA, CAGS, CPA
Jim is the Partner responsible for Coopers & Lybrand's National SAP practice based in Valley Forge, Pennsylvania. He has a strong background in applying technology to business with C&L and other Big 6 consultancies. He has been implementing SAP R/3 in North America since 1993.

Grant Norris, BS, MBA
Grant is a Senior Director in Coopers & Lybrand's National SAP practice. He has worked in designing and installing enterprise systems for a variety of organizations in Canada, Europe, the Middle East, and the United States. He has been implementing SAP software since 1988.

Alison Gibson, MA, CMA
Alison is a Manager in Coopers & Lybrand's Integrated Strategic Services practice based in Philadelphia, Pennsylvania. She has experience in designing and installing information systems and now specializes in IT strategy.

She has worked in the installation and selection of SAP software in Europe, North America, and the Pacific Rim since 1988.

Ian Wright, BS

Ian is a Manager in Coopers & Lybrand's National SAP practice. His background is in designing and installing financial systems with C&L and other major consulting firms. He has worked with SAP software in Europe and North America since 1990.

Foreword

These are exciting and challenging times. Every day we jump hurdles we could not have foreseen ten years ago. Global organizations are becoming the norm and we are faced with providing 100 percent customer satisfaction to a wide range of needs. To do this, we are establishing Best-In-Class business processes and corporate infrastructures to support them. At the same time, technology options are changing daily. Converging business needs with available technologies is our greatest challenge today. Those organizations that do this successfully will be the ones to thrive in the twenty-first century. Those individuals who spearhead this change within their own organizations are the ones who will lead in the years ahead. Unfortunately, success is not easy.

Today we have tools to help us in our work. SAP has emerged as the leading enterprise resources planning solution for transforming today's business. Effectively migrating your organization to SAP is a complex task. Costs, expectations, people, and technology must be simultaneously managed through significant change to ensure success. This must be done at the same time as continuing to run a profitable business. Deploying SAP has been likened to changing a tire on a moving car. In this case, the job of managing an SAP deployment is like doing it in the dark. It's hard to know what to do, when to do it, and exactly what is happening at any one time. Simply put — it's not easy. However, if done correctly, success for both the organizations and individuals involved can be the end result.

To be successful at transforming a business, the organization's leadership must understand why it needs to change and agree to invest in the change. How much change is needed and the extent of the investment are questions that are difficult to answer. Equally as difficult is aligning the organization to accept and take on the change. This involves being clear about what functions are changing, when they will change, and the nature of the change itself. When SAP is the enabling technology, specialized knowledge and insight are required to provide this information to both the leadership and the rest of the organization.

Jack Dunleavy, Jim Hurley, Grant Norris, Alison Gibson, and Ian Wright have done an excellent job at providing a framework that can be used to understand how SAP can impact your organization. For the executive, they have provided a clear introduction to SAP, which includes guidance on how SAP could impact your core business processes, typical expectations, and information on how large an investment may be required. They discuss how a company could determine if they are even "ready and able" to implement SAP. This is a key question if you are the one who must sign off on significant SAP-related expenditures. For those interested in more detail, they discuss overall methodological processes for SAP, tools, program management approaches that work, change management and even how to pick a consulting organization that suits you. They provide sensible, practical advice on how to be successful in implementing SAP.

I have had the privilege of working with the authors of this book for a number of years, as both a consultant and in my role as the CIO of Lucent Technologies. I know that my clients and Lucent have benefited significantly from their industry and SAP expertise. Their knowledge, contained in this book, is based on more than 50 years of combined SAP and industry experience. It is an invaluable aid to anyone undertaking the challenge of implementing SAP and/or transforming their core business processes. Any reader, from a seasoned executive to a recent graduate, should read this book if he or she is either involved in, or thinking about being involved in, such an exercise.

This book casts light on how to change your business process and support the change with SAP. Reading it can help to ensure your own success by learning how to get the most out of your investment in SAP. Hopefully, you too will be one of those individuals and organizations thriving in the twenty-first century.

> Herbert G. Vinnicombe
> Vice President & Chief Information Officer
> Lucent Technologies

Preface

Dozens of books have been written about how to implement SAP's software. We have found, as we talk to company executives about why their companies might want to install SAP's R/3 software and about how we might help them to do so, a lack of understanding about exactly what the software does, how it works, and exactly what advantages it offers to businesses that complete a successful implementation.

We have determined from these discussions that there is a need for a book that explains, first to executives, and later to those who are positioned as the management leaders of the implementation effort itself, how integrated software solutions—what we call Enterprise Resource Planning (ERP) solutions—can be used to meet the business challenges of today and tomorrow. We define an ERP software solutions as a fully integrated, full-service suite of software.

Our book is a team effort, based on our experiences in the real world of SAP implementations, from a high-level consulting perspective. We say that because team members come from a variety of backgrounds, in general management, strategic planning, auditing, and systems development. Wherever our origins, we have all worked for many years at the level where consultants help teams, project managers, and program managers to manage overall implementation efforts.

We have all seen implementation efforts that have gone well, and we have all seen those that have gone poorly. However, we have come to a point in our careers where we are in agreement that the greatest risks to a company in an SAP R/3 implementation are organizational risks, not technical or marketplace risks.

This book is written for businesspeople, be they chief executive officers, finance executives, information technology executives or operations executives. It is an introduction for the uninitiated, which presents a look at some of the major trends affecting business today and how SAP software can be used to effectively manage business in that environment.

The book is also useful for information systems staff in introducing them to some of the business issues that general managers and system users are facing and some of the solutions they are looking for from the ERP system.

Finally, the book is also for front-line implementors—program managers, project managers, and implementation team members. In addition to introducing them to SAP and the software, the book also looks at some of the workplace and organizational dynamics issues they will face during the implementation.

INTEGRATED SOLUTIONS AND IMPLEMENTATION

Integrated solutions are large; they cover multiple business applications. More often than not, they require change in the underlying business processes in order to be fully successful.

Some people view them as a cost, often as a waste of money; others view them as an investment that is necessary in order to compete in a rapidly changing business environment.

Because these software solutions are large, they are complex to implement. They are complex not merely because of the size—the number of users who will use the system—but more so because of scope—the fact that those users cut across numerous functions within the company.

For years, many consultants—Coopers & Lybrand, L.L.P. at the forefront—have spoken and written about business process redesign as an effort to make operational processes more effective, not merely efficient. Our colleagues have argued that information technology should not be the driver of redesign, but rather should be used as an enabler of the process redesign effort.

Though they knew what they wanted this enabling technology to do for business managers in their efforts to run redesigned and streamlined business processes, their colleagues in the information technology arena could not build systems fast enough that had the size, depth, and breadth necessary. Until off-the-shelf ERP solution software was developed, the only way to achieve the functionality we today find in SAP's R/3 software and its competitors was to custom-design it. Because many in-house information technology (IT) groups often designed for system elegance rather than ease of use, the disconnect between the business managers and the IT group continued.

It has really been only in the last couple of years, with the advent of R/3 technology, that companies have truly been able to use off-the-shelf information systems as enabling technology in a business process redesign effort.

That is a key to two of our central arguments in this book. First, SAP software (or that of its ERP competitors—Baan, J.D. Edwards, PeopleSoft, and Oracle) is not, in and of itself, able to provide a company with a competitive advantage. Using ERP software, however, companies are now able to truly re-engineer those processes that might lead to competitive advantage. This is an important distinction, especially for those in the executive suite.

Second, and building from the first, ERP software is a cost, and possibly a waste of money, unless it is installed properly so that it can be used to its fullest potential. Only when installed properly, with the requisite business process change, project and program management, and proper management of the necessary workplace change does ERP software become an investment.

This book does not seek to sell a product or a service per se. However, we do believe we look at the implementation effort in a different way than many other consulting firms that work as SAP partners. If you appreciate our point of view in these matters, we would certainly welcome speaking with you further about your own implementation effort.

Acknowledgments

This is a book written by management consultants. We have been working with SAP for many years and in many countries. Throughout this time, we have had the privilege to work with many project teams and learn from a large number of talented people. As such, this book represents the experience of not only the five authors but also that of the project teams we've worked with.

There are too many individuals to name, but our special thanks go to all the partners and staff of Coopers & Lybrand's Information/Communications, Information Strategy, and National SAP practices.

Our thanks also go to Eileen Peat and Sandie Pratt for their patience and support in helping us administer the project and decipher our handwritten notes and diagrams. Only those who know us can truly appreciate what this means.

It is impossible to underestimate the contribution of Jon Zonderman in writing this book. He listened to our thoughts and discussions, tolerated our meeting schedules, and kept his patience and humor. Thank you, Jon, for everything you did.

Finally, our thanks go to all our families, who have not only tolerated the years of late nights, travel and absence, but supported us through the weekend work, trials, and tribulations of producing this manuscript. Without their patience, support, and understanding none of this would have been possible.

To all of the above, we express our deepest gratitude.

Contents

Contents

Contents

Part I

The Executive View

In this first section, we take the executive through a general discussion of enterprise resource planning (ERP) software in general and the SAP company in particular.

Too often we find in preliminary discussions with companies seeking assistance in implementing SAP R/3 that the decision to proceed with the implementation has been made without a full discussion of a number of critical issues. Those issues include the organizational implications of such a large change effort and the cost to the company in cash, time, and *personpower* that the effort will entail.

Even more than the effects of the implementation itself, we sometimes find that companies go into an ERP implementation with those in the executive suite not truly understanding what the software is designed to do, and what it cannot and will not do.

In the chapters in this part, we put the horse in front of the cart, the way it ought to be. We begin with a look at the company, its history, and its goals in software design. Then, we discuss the need to conduct a thorough information systems and technology strategy formulation and create a business case for implementing ERP software.

Only then do we discuss the organizational effects that such a massive undertaking will have, first on the finance organization, then on the manufacturing, distribution, and sales organizations. While SAP and other ERP software providers work in the realm of information technology (IT), the effects on the company are more widespread and more profound in areas other than Information Technology.

1

Who Is SAP, and What Is R/3?

Suddenly, it seems, the letters SAP are ubiquitous. They appear almost daily on the back page of the *New York Times* business section. They are heard on public radio as sponsors of news and cultural broadcasts. They are on the upturned brim of the golfer Jasper Parnevik's cap.

The advertisement boasts that nine of 10 of America's largest companies use SAP software, that eight of 10 of the most profitable American companies use it; that thousands of Windows NT users use it.

Who is this company, which has suddenly exploded onto the American scene? What does it provide? Can its bravado be reconciled with reality? And how is it pronounced?

The company is called S-A-P, not sap, which comes from trees. The software the company sells, which is designed to integrate business operations, is not called SAP. One doesn't buy SAP, one buys SAP's R/2 or R/3 software.

SAP AT 25

In 1972, five German IBM programmers left the company and began *Systemanalyse und Programmentwicklung* (Systems Analysis and Program Development), a company that did contract software development for businesses using IBM mainframes. To be sure, these were not the only IBMers who left Big Blue to pursue their own business interests. Most purchasers of mainframes in those days hired contract programmers to assist their own data processing departments develop custom codes for their business.

By the late 1970s, some of these contract software providers were beginning to ask: "Why build every system from scratch?" In the United States such providers as McCormack and Dodge and Computer Associates began putting the best pieces they had designed for clients into packaged business software and selling it as *application software*, meaning that the software performed a particular business application (such as general ledger or inventory) or a set of applications.

SAP's first product in this market was R/2, released in 1979. The company by this time had become a GmbH (a closely held company) and changed its name to *Systeme, Anwendungen, Produckte in der Datenverarbeitung* (Systems Applications and Products in Data Processing).

The idea behind R/2 was somewhat novel; to move from batch processing by the data processing (DP) department to real-time, on-line processing in which the computer screen (more likely a dumb terminal screen) becomes the focus of data processing. In addition, the company sought to create a standard business software product that integrates all business data processing.

Within a year, the company had sold licenses to use its product to every major German corporation and the company began to look to international markets. In 1987, the company announced its strategy to develop the R/3 product (the product in use today) and a year later floated a public offering of stock, becoming SAP AG. R/3 was released early in 1992 in Europe and in November 1992 in the United States. In early 1998, Release 4.0 of R/3 was launched.

Today, SAP is the fifth largest software vendor in the world and the market leader in Enterprise Resource Planning (ERP) software, sometimes known as Administrative Applications Software (AAS), according to International Data Corporation. The company has 6,000 customers worldwide, with R/3 installed in 9,000 business unit or corporate sites, and R/2 in another 2,000. The company had revenues of over $2.4 billion in 1996, with 75 percent coming from outside Germany.

Most long-time clients are in the production industries, although the company is now expanding into the service industries by creating industry solution software, a set of industry-specific modules that enhance the basic software. The company still has few financial services clients.

R/2 AND R/3: THE HIGHLIGHTS

At their most basic, both R/2 and R/3 are truly integrated suites of application software modules for business processes from manufacturing to back-office functions such as order processing. Exhibit 1.1 shows a typical legacy system environment for order taking, with many functional systems linked by "black box" interfaces.

In an SAP environment, as shown in Exhibit 1.2, the need for interfaces is eliminated, greatly simplifying the task of reconciliation and audit.

Both software programs use real-time database updates and are designed to support organizations with multiple companies and locations.

Exhibit 1.1   Traditional Architecture

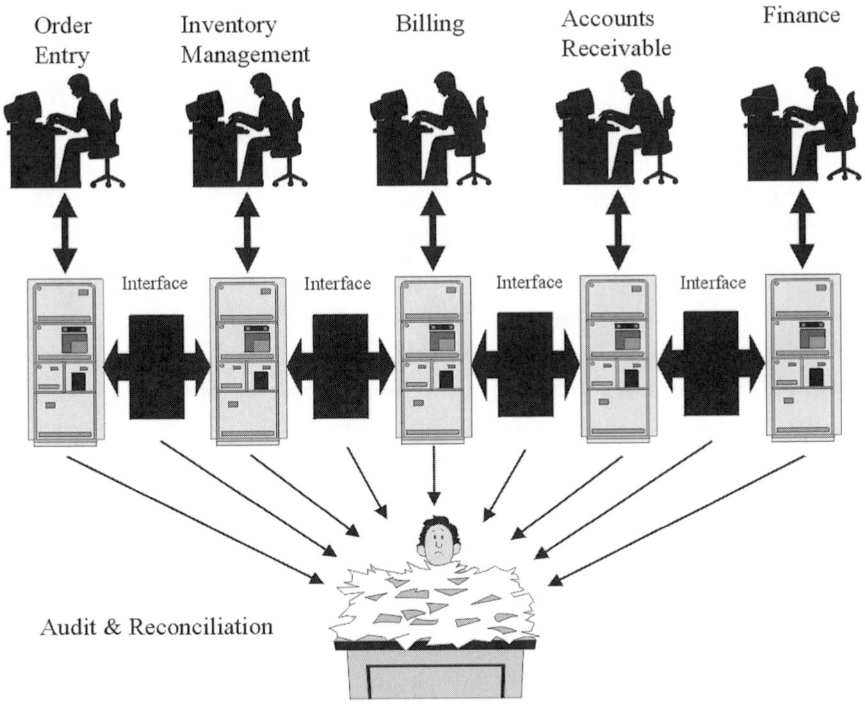

Exhibit 1.2   SAP Architecture

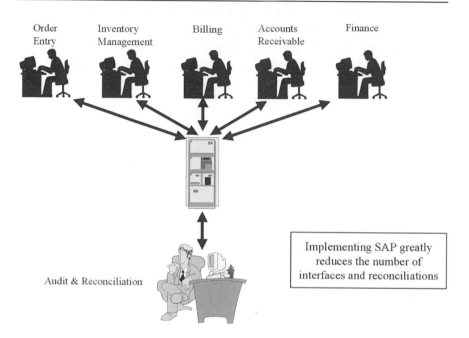

Order   Inventory   Billing   Accounts   Finance
Entry   Management   Receivable

Audit & Reconciliation

Implementing SAP greatly
reduces the number of
interfaces and reconciliations

They allow for multilanguage and multicurrency use, and are written in their own programming language, advanced business application programming (ABAP/4).

The two products differ in a number of key areas, however.

R/2 is a mainframe product. It does some batch processing and works best in environments with high transaction volumes.

Currently, R/2 Release 5.0 is in use. Release 6.0 is under development and will allow for Internet capabilities and some distributed computing architecture.

R/3, however, is used primarily in a client–server environment in which a host computer holds data files and client computers bring the files out of the host to use them, then return them to the host when they are done. R/3 is capable of being run on a centralized mainframe, but few companies use it this way. R/3 has a true graphic user interface (windows and icons rather than written menus). Within R/3, there is an increasing number of individual industry solution modules.

The biggest difference in terms of operations is that R/2 must be taken off line to run batch processing. With R/3, a company can keep its computer operations running 24 hours a day, seven days a week.

WHY YOU MIGHT CONSIDER INSTALLING R/3 IN YOUR BUSINESS

There are a few reasons you may consider SAP's R/3 for your company. It is important to look at these reasons and ask oneself if they are really the right reasons for undergoing the time, effort, and expense it will take to properly undertake the installation of SAP software and the organizational changes necessary to get the most out of the software.

- ○ You are engaging in a business process re-engineering (BPR) effort and have heard that one can "kill two birds with one stone" by installing SAP R/3 now.

  This is a good reason. As will be discussed in detail in much of Part One, an SAP software installation and a business process re-engineering effort go hand in hand.

- ○ You think this will be a quicker, easier, and less costly fix to your "Year 2000" problem than upgrading current systems.

  This is not a very good reason. Unless your organization is small—under $250 million in annual revenue—and has only simple processes, it is already too late. In fact, properly installing SAP software in your company will probably take as much time, be as difficult, and cost as much, as upgrading your current legacy systems. Because there are hundreds (if not thousands) of companies going through the same decision process you are, it will be just as hard to find the necessary human resources to either hire or bring in as consultants either way.

- ○ It is part of a well-thought-out information technology strategy. Your company has aging IT architecture; runaway selling, general, and administrative (SG&A) costs; or both.

  We're all for IT strategy. In Chapter 2, we'll discuss in some detail the kind of IT strategy exercise you should go through before you make a decision whether to upgrade or move to another software solution, and whether that solution should be SAP's software or something else. Many companies installing SAP are finding that their SG&A costs can be reduced by orders of magnitude.

○ You think you can get a jump on your competitors.

This is the "SAP software as business strategy" reason. In and of itself, it is probably not a very good strategy. ERP software really doesn't get at your company's core business processes, which is what gives you any competitive advantage you have. Rather, ERP software adds efficiency to much of your back-office operations, thereby freeing up managerial and executive time to concentrate on developing your company's core competencies and capabilities, and giving your company competitive advantage. To get the full benefit of the software in a business strategy sense, the installation should be coupled with process enhancement work and building of competencies and capabilities.

○ Your competitors have SAP software and you feel you must "keep up with the Joneses." Or your cash-rich chief information officer (CIO) who thinks it would be cool to move from a mainframe to a client–server environment.

To some degree, this is the flip side of the previous reason. Again, unless you are willing to spend the time doing the installation right, including the necessary process enhancement, organization and culture changes, you will continue to chase those competitors that have done it right. ERP software is not a magic bullet for poor business strategy or for poor execution of that business strategy. Many CIOs who like the bells and whistles are finding, during installation implementation, that the business reasons for taking on an SAP software installation are as compelling as the technology itself.

○ You can't get fired recommending SAP.

Unfortunately, part of SAP's becoming the 600-pound gorilla of the ERP software world is that too many business unit or divisional executives are taking on an installation of the software on the advice of their chief financial officer (CFO) or CIO without understanding what they are getting into. They then get authority from the corporate level, where again too many executives are not as familiar with the details as they should be. No one gets fired for recommending the industry leader.

However, when the inevitable problems occur during installation—the inevitable problems of culture change and process re-engineering—people who made the recommendations get fired for not delivering.

Exhibit 1.3 provides reasons why a corporation may select SAP.

Exhibit 1.3   Why SAP?

 As part of a BPR effort

 Year 2000 Solution

 As part of an IT Strategy

 To get a jump on competitors

 Keeping up with the Joneses

 You can't get fired for it

SAP'S STRATEGY

The company's strategy for penetrating an increasingly global market and for moving beyond corporate giants to mid-sized companies ($250 million to $2 billion) is fairly straightforward.

First, R/3, to a greater extent than R/2, has penetrated the market-place of global organizations by capturing a number of clients among U.S. companies. Both R/2 and R/3 have the ability to be used by individuals speaking different languages sitting next to each other. R/3 also does multicurrency computations and parallel currency computations for companies operating in countries with high inflation.

R/3 is platform independent, not bound to any one hardware, database, or operating system environment. It runs primarily on client–server based systems and has the flexibility to work on a multitiered client server, that is, one that has databases at one level, applications housed at another level, and presentation at a third level. It is infinitely scalable, meaning that a customer can build a distributed system as large and broad as it desires.

SAP is developing capabilities for clients to utilize JAVA programming language, which will allow R/3 to run on a wider range of less expensive hardware platforms. Already, the company has created an implementation methodology for smaller client installations on hardware such as AS/400s.

The software itself focuses on information needed in the key business applications, such as general ledger, accounts payable, order entry, and so forth, and allows for "bolt ons" of applications for noncore processes. For instance, in the area of finance, R/3 has modules in financial accounting, controlling, asset management, and treasury and capital investment management. However, it does not have a module for other areas such as U.S. sales and use tax.

Admitting that it does not have expertise in all areas, and that there are products available that it does not wish to put resources into competing against, SAP forms partnerships with third-party software developers to link their applications to R/3. Examples of such agreements are Vertex (sales and use tax), Microsoft, and I2. (Chapter 21 details third-party tools and bolt-on modules.)

SAP seeks to increase flexibility with each new release of its products. Release 4.0 has the ability to work with distributed systems, as well as the ability to work on the Internet and intranets. The company's products have a reputation as the best integrated, although not every module has the reputation as the best product for that specific application.

In addition, the company is working to reduce implementation time to get R/3 up and running, especially for smaller clients. It has created some tools, licensed third-party tools, and created an implementation methodology called Accelerated SAP (ASAP).

Exhibit 1.4   SAP in the Press

The press has been somewhat fickle in its coverage of SAP. On the one hand are the hype-type stories about the company, and on the other hand are the horror stories about "failures" of implementation. Exhibit 1.4 shows some of the more lurid headlines from the general and trade press.

WHY IS SAP SO SUCCESSFUL?

There are a number of theories as to why SAP has been and continues to be so successful.

One is that it simply "caught the wave" of application software, being in the right place at the right time, and has become the "phenomenon" of the software industry like Michael Jordan in basketball or the Beatles in pop music. To be sure, the company has generated cash and stayed cash rich; the company has had and maintains strong financial results and an ability to execute its business vision.

A second is that its heavy investment in research and development (R&D)—17 percent of revenue—has kept it one step ahead of the pack.

(The company had been spending 25 percent of revenue on R&D, but the revenue got so large—$2.4 billion in 1996—that it couldn't find ways to spend 25 percent on R&D.) The company has a keen knowledge of business and how business processes are integrated within the enterprise, across enterprises, and within the Internet or intranets.

A third is that its culture, the European model of working together, has allowed it to create a network of partnerships with service providers such as consultants and third-party application developers, as well as a "partnering" relationship with its clients, that is uniquely suited to enterprise-wide business solutions and long-term commitment to those solutions. SAP "hooked" all of the Big 6 accounting/consulting firms, as well as the second-tier firms, by offering free training so they could develop practices in SAP implementation consulting.*

IS SAP IN YOUR FUTURE?

While some are predicting that SAP's day in the sun is almost over, it seems that the company will dominate for several more years, and that with its large installed base and its tradition of service and upgrades, it should be a viable company well into the future.

Although the company may not be the leader in Internet applications, which are becoming increasingly important, it is in the market, working to develop ways for its licensees to use the Internet. In effect, SAP's software can be an "on ramp" to the Internet for an organization, giving companies a way to truly make money from the Internet.

If a company could take orders over the Internet and have those orders feed into its ERP software, it could do away with the front end of the order-entry process, the order taker who inputs the order into the system. In effect, customers would be their own order-entry persons. In the same way McDonald's and other fast-food restaurants shifted the burden of busing tables to the customer, companies could shift the burden of order entry to their customers using the Internet and their ERP software.

Implementation costs and time lines have in the past been the company's most difficult problems to overcome and the source of much public

* In the interest of full disclosure, Coopers & Lybrand is an SAP partner, and the authors of this book have all undergone training in SAP's software.

criticism. However, both costs and time for implementation are falling. This is happening slowly for larger companies and larger implementations, as those who assist with these implementations increase their own knowledge; and rapidly for smaller companies and smaller implementations, most notably due to SAP's fast-track methodology, Accelerated SAP (ASAP).

Part of the reason for this is the changing role of consultants and implementors. SAP installations are being linked more explicitly with business re-engineering efforts. R/2 consultants were basically coders who configured 100 or more tables to give the client the format desired. Today, there are tools that do much of the system configuration for you.

Consultants working with R/3 installations need to work with companies to change processes and change businesses in order to get the full power out of an SAP R/3 installation. This means skills in project management and change management, as well as technical and business skills. The front-end cost for this kind of installation may be high, but by putting the process and change in place, the installation runs more smoothly and back-end consulting costs are lower.

2

What Is The Business Case for Implementing SAP Software?

In Chapter 1, six reasons were suggested for why a company may be looking toward an SAP software installation. Some of those reasons were good ones, while others were not so good. The best reason, clearly, is that using SAP software is a conscious decision one has come to after putting together a comprehensive information technology (IT) strategy; determining the need for an enterprise resource planning (ERP) solution; understanding the trends in both business and technology that lead one to that determination; and, finally, building the business case for SAP rather than one of its competitors. This chapter will take you through that decision-making process.

Exhibit 2.1 shows the "by-the-book" progression of IT implementation. In this chapter, the focus will be on the first two pieces of the chain: the strategic plan and the solution selection.

BEGIN WITH INFORMATION TECHNOLOGY STRATEGY

In order to build a sound IT strategy, you must first understand your company's business strategy. Then, an IT strategy can be built in the context of the business strategy.

Exhibit 2.1   Key Activities in the System Life Cycle

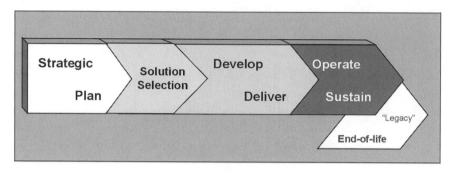

Key Activities in IT Plan Development and Solutions Selection

- *Business alignment*
- *Business modeling*
- *Assessment and review*
- *Architecture formulation*
- *Investment justification*
- *Implementation planning*

Information technology strategy is the alignment of the information technology infrastructure and investment with the business's strategic direction. An IT strategic plan details how IT will be used to support the business, specifically:

- ○ What technology will be deployed and where
- ○ What the system's architecture will look like
- ○ What software applications will be utilized
- ○ How the IT staff will be organized
- ○ What investments are required to bring the IT infrastructure up to the level envisioned in the plan

Just as it is said that war is too important to be left to generals, IT strategy is too important to be left to chief information officers (CIOs) and their staffs. A company's IT strategy development process must include input from the chief executive officer (CEO) and the key business executives if it is to enable the business strategy, rather than merely being a collection of the newest and coolest in technological wizardry.

The IT strategy development process typically spawns a number of implementation projects, of which installation of SAP software may be one. Investments in dollars, time, people, and other resources must be justified first in terms of anticipated financial payback and then in terms of ancillary organizational benefits.

Some companies are more organized about their IT strategic development than others. A few companies routinely initiate an IT strategic assessment every two or three years. Other companies have a continuous, "rolling" IT strategic assessment.

Most companies, however, conduct an IT strategic assessment in a more ad hoc manner, either in response to a specific business event; in response to constant lobbying by the CIO or internal consultants; or as part of an assessment carried out by an external consultant, who may be brought into the organization for a very different reason but say, "You really need to look at your information technology abilities concurrent with this other effort we are carrying out."

Some of the specific business events and trends that are driving companies today to undertake IT strategic assessments are as follows:

- Year 2000 issues
- Merger or acquisition
- Part of the business process redesign effort
- In response to a comment from the company's auditor
- Need for reduce selling, general, and administrative (SG&A) expenses
- In response to a benchmark against competitors

These trends will be discussed in more detail in the section entitled Building the Business Case.

An IT strategic assessment, and the IT strategy derived from it, take into account all aspects of the company's information storage, retrieval, transmission, and computational capabilities, including local area networks (LANs), personal computers (PCs) and the software that runs on them, wide area networks (WANs) and other telecommunications technology, business systems hardware, and business applications software (of which SAP's software is a specific example).

Exhibit 2.2   An Organization's IT Thought Process

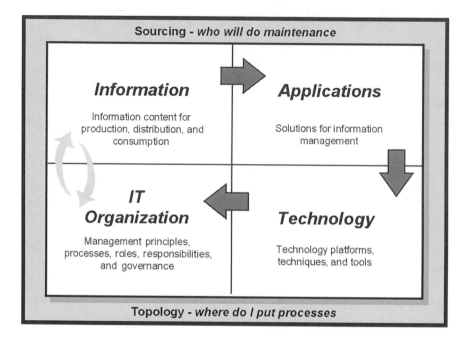

Exhibit 2.2 shows the typical flow of thought in a holistic view of IT. First, one should think about information and ask a number of questions:

o What is it?
o Where does information come from?
o How do we create information from data?
o How does information get distributed?
o How does information get consumed?

These lead inherently to questions about software, since that is the level at which most information providers or users interact with the IT system. The following questions are asked here:

o What applications does the company currently use to collect data, collate it, compute it and imbue it with meaning (transforming data into usable information), distribute and finally consume that information?

○ Is there better application software available to carry out these tasks in a more efficient, less time-consuming, less resource-consuming, and less expensive way? By using these new applications, could the company redirect resources into other areas of the business in which it can establish competitive advantage?

At this point, the discussion of hardware begins. Here is where most people in the organization (even at the executive level) drop out of the discussion. This is the discussion about technology platforms, techniques, and tools. This is where SAP the company, as a provider of ERP software, has excelled, making its software essentially platform independent.

Finally, after the discussion of hardware, comes the discussion about the IT staff's internal organization. Unfortunately, since many executives have dropped out of the discussion at the hardware stage, they don't re-assert themselves into the organization discussion, which they should. The following are key questions in this part of the discussion:

○ What *management principles* will govern the IT organization? Management principles refer to the guiding rules of the organization and the reporting mechanisms within the organization.

○ What *processes* are used? These are processes for system development, operations, and user support.

○ What are the various *roles and responsibilities* of all the individuals within the organization?

○ What is the method of *governance* in the organization? Governance refers to the power structure and relationship between the IT organization and the business operating units. Governance helps determine the issue resolution process.

KEY THEMES OF CONCERN TO THE CHIEF INFORMATION OFFICER

The CIO has five key concerns as we near the twenty-first century:

1. Do my systems have "Year 2000" problems? If yes, how do I solve them?

2. How can I reduce my IT costs? Should I look to oursourcing or to a turnkey solution? Is there another option?
3. Should the company be using a centralized or a decentralized architecture?
4. What should we be doing with regard to Internet commerce?
5. Should we be setting up a data warehouse, and can we use data mining techniques?

Year 2000

Having determined the magnitude and extent of the risk within an organization, a CIO is faced with three basic options: The Information Technology organization can basically live with the problem, implementing temporary workarounds; it can upgrade its existing systems by modifying source code; or it can replace old systems with Year 2000 compliant systems, of which SAP is an example.

With less than two full years to go before Year 2000 D-day, it is safe to say that, for most companies, if they haven't already made a decision and started down a particular path, their options are essentially cut to the first. In other words, for most companies, it's too late to try to install a new, Year 2000–compliant system.

We hedge this a bit, because smaller companies with less complex business processes can possibly implement SAP R/3 in response to Year 2000 concerns. Using SAP's Accelerated SAP (ASAP) methodology, it is possible to get the system up and running in six months if the company is willing to do it with a minimum of process re-engineering and human resources "change management," and if the SAP expertise can be found in the marketplace.

Information Technology Costs

Chief Information Officers face increasing pressure to reduce the total expenditure on IT as part of total SG&A costs. Outsourcing of systems operations is one option. Outsourcing provides significant potential for reducing costs. Providers of outsourced services usually have offerings in the areas of operation and maintenance of mainframe-based systems, server/PC desktop support, and WAN/LAN support.

Outsourcing a live SAP system is not a good strategy. To do so means surrendering control of key operational business systems. Outsourcing of legacy systems operations has, however, been used as a temporary measure to enable IT organizations to focus on building a new SAP system.

Chief Information Officers may also wish to consider the option of a turnkey applications development strategy, which involves handing over the design, building, and implementation of new applications to a third party.

We also caution against the use of a turnkey solution with SAP. It is important that an organization be intimately involved with the development of what will ultimately become one of its core business systems.

Architecture

The current trend in IT architecture is away from a centralized mainframe powerhouse accessed by dumb terminals and toward a distributed client–server architecture, which harnesses the power of desktop computing. SAP is compliant with this trend. Release 3.0 (R/3) supports a three-tier client–server architecture (applications on one server, data potentially on a second, and presentation on the desktop). Release 4.0 (R/4) allows applications to be distributed between multiple servers.

Internet Commerce

It is possible to build SAP transactions that can be run from a web page (which may be part of the Internet, or part of an organization's intranet). Examples of where this could be useful are order entry, order tracking, and purchase requisitioning.

Data Warehousing and Data Mining

A data warehouse is the store of vast quantities of data for future analysis. Data mining is the process of extracting useful data from this enormous warehouse and is currently used most often in the area of marketing and vendor management.

SAP stores key operational information, such as sales, customers, and so on. Release 4.0 introduces SAP's native data mining facility, called BIW (business information warehouse), which allows the extraction of potentially useful data to a separate data warehouse that can subsequently be mined.

WHAT IS ERP SOFTWARE AND WHY WOULD IT BENEFIT A COMPANY?

Enterprise Resource Planning is a term used to describe business software that is:

- o Multifunctional in scope—it tracks financial results (dollars), procurement (material), sales (people and goods) and manufacturing (people and resources)
- o Integrated in nature, that is, when a piece of data is entered regarding one of the functions, data regarding the other functions is changed
- o Modular in structure, that is, it can be used in a way that is as expansive or narrow as you choose

SAP is an example of an ERP software package.

An ERP software solution is appropriate when an organization is seeking the benefits of integration and contemporary best practices in its information system, looking for a full range of functionality from the back office through operations and sales, and seeking to limit its implementation and ongoing support cost.

An ERP solution can be "built," using many pieces of software from different vendors, or can be purchased as a package from a single vendor, such as SAP. The tradeoff is fairly simple. A multivendor solution, while giving a company the opportunity to purchase the "best in class" of each module, may mean increased cost and increased resources needed to implement. A single-vendor, packaged ERP solution, however, may ease the implementation strains, but the functionality and features available in any particular area may not be the best available, although the package may contain all that is needed in every module. The question is really one of local optimization of each module, or global optimization of a multimodule package.

The following are key considerations to think about when an ERP software package is being selected:

- o The complexity of the business, including the degree of vertical integration and the level of international operations
- o The size of the business, in revenue

- o The scope of the functionality needed (i.e., do you want to be able to look at sales data or manufacturing? If manufacturing is to be included, do you operate in a discreet manufacturing environment or process manufacturing, or a mixture?)
- o The degree of sophistication and unique requirements in the company's future business process (Are there unique customer information requirements or ways that are needed to cut and present information? In short, how much of a custom solution is needed?)
- o The budget for the implementation
- o The hardware considerations, if any (Is there an existing hardware platform the company wants or needs to stay with? Is there a particular platform the company wishes to move to?)

The answers to all of these questions should be included in the request for proposals (RFPs) issued to vendors. The more information provided to vendors up front, the more focused proposals can be, the quicker the project can get started, and the smoother the implementation can run.

DISTINGUISHING FEATURES OF SAP

Within the realm of single-vendor ERP solutions, SAP software has a number of distinguishing features.

First, it has the broadest and deepest available functionality. Most organizations utilize only 20 percent of R/3's available functionality. Despite this, SAP clients have the ability to choose from a larger menu of available functionality than clients of any other software provider. The 20 percent of functionality one SAP client uses may be very much different from the 20 percent of functionality another client uses.

R/3 also offers full integration of manufacturing, customer-facing, and back-office functions in real time and in a seamless way.

Finally, R/3 is a truly global product, with preferences defined by user in terms of currency and language. Increasingly, SAP is coming up with industry solutions, which allows a user to semi-customize the software to better fit the industry environment in which the client does business.

Historically, R/3 has been successfully used predominantly by large, multinational manufacturing companies (revenues over $1 billion) that operate in a discreet manufacturing environment, as well as by companies in the process chemicals industry that are primarily seeking back-office software.

Today, however, SAP is consciously trying to gain clients among mid-sized companies ($250 million to $1 billion) and small companies (under $250 million).

Specific industry solutions, a new version of R/3 based on AS/400 technology, and its in-house implementation methodology, ASAP, all help to aim the company's efforts at smaller companies. The rapid implementation methodology is aimed at "vanilla" businesses, defined as (1) having a low degree of process specialization, (2) having basic financial management reporting requirements only, (3) having a willingness to adopt standard SAP practices throughout the business, and (4) having the ability to make pragmatic decisions rapidly.

SAP believes these kinds of companies can implement a full installation of R/3 software in six to nine months, while larger, more unwieldy companies often take 12 to 18 months and sometimes more to fully implement the software.

BUILDING THE BUSINESS CASE

After completing a detailed IT strategic assessment and developing an IT strategic plan, and after determining that an ERP solution is right for the company, it is time to build the business case. This involves analyzing costs and benefits, determining the payback period for the expenses incurred in the implementation, and getting all of the necessary corporate approvals.

Exhibit 2.3 shows how the complexity of the implementation, as well as the project risk and cost, increases as a company moves out on the continuum of the degree of business process change and up along the continuum of organizational change. These two axes work hand in glove: As the level of business process change is increased, the level of organizational change necessary to carry it out must also increase.

Exhibit 2.4 gives an idea of the time frame for implementation that should realistically be expected, depending on the level of business process change being undertaken and the complexity of the underlying business.

These illustrations suggest the need for caution in a company's expectations of any implementation of SAP software. It is important to un-

Exhibit 2.3　Complexity Increases with Increased Process Change

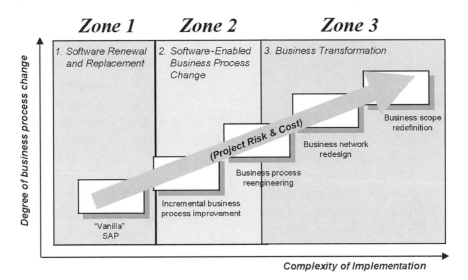

Exhibit 2.4　Approximate Time Frames for Process Change

Degree of Business Process Change

		Zone 1 Low	Zone 2 Medium	Zone 3 High
Business Complexity	**High**	12 – 18 months	18 – 36 months	24 – 48+ months
	Medium	6 – 9 months	12 – 18 months	18 – 36 months
	Low **(Vanilla SAP)**	3 – 6 months	6 – 9 months	12 – 18 months

derstand that *the further along in the implementation the company moves, the more it will be pulled toward business process change.* What starts out as an implementation in which the business leaders believe that their organization is in zone 2 can be pulled into zone 3 over time.

That is the reason BPR is considered as straddling the line. When a company begins a BPR effort and coincident SAP R/3 installation, the business leaders may believe that the company is in zone 2, but find that the processes are being transformed more radically than they thought, increasing the degree of organizational change necessary and also increasing the cost, time, and ultimate risk.

A lot of press coverage tends to focus on SAP implementation projects as complex, difficult, and frequently behind schedule and over budget. However, there have been a number of successful projects delivered on time and on budget. The blame for failures is often put on SAP and the software, when the blame for most delayed or canceled projects should be put on the inability of the company to understand large-scale business process change efforts, and especially the organizational change component of those efforts.

The key to successful implementation is assertive control over the project's scope and over the degree of business process change to be undertaken. A good analogy for the inability to control project scope is the spring cleaning project, especially the one carried out by a man in the garage, the basement, the attic, or the toolshed.

For example, you decide to clean the garage, so you start pulling things off the shelves in order to clean the shelving. The cutting tools up there need to be sharpened, so you begin on that task. Then, while you have the grinding stone out, you decide that you ought to sharpen the lawnmower blade as well. While you're taking the lawn mower apart, you figure you should change the oil and the oil filter and the spark plug. This means a trip to the store for parts.

By the end of the day, all of the gardening equipment may be clean, sharp, and in fine working order, but there are still cobwebs hanging from the ceiling, the floor is still filthy, and the shelving is still full of things that should have been thrown away. You're over budget and late in delivering a clean garage.

BUSINESS CASE ESSENTIALS

There are several key points to remember as a company moves toward acquiring and implementing ERP solution software.

- o The decision must be driven by business considerations, not merely by the desire to be out front technologically.
- o An ERP solution will not solve business process and organizational dynamic problems. In fact, ERP software tends to highlight these problems, which means they must be dealt with before or coincidental with implementing an ERP solution.
- o Implementation of an ERP solution cannot be delayed until the company is able to use it to its fullest. The scope of the initial installation must be determined and installation carried out. Then, the company will grow into its ERP system over time.

3

How Will an SAP R/3 Implementation Affect Finance Organizations?

In Chapter 2, some of the business trends affecting large and increasingly global corporations were briefly discussed.

In this chapter and Chapter 4, how implementing SAP R/3 software affects an organization in light of these trends will be discussed in more detail. This chapter will look specifically at how the implementation affects the chief financial officer (CFO) and the entire finance organization, while Chapter 4 will cover how an SAP implementation affects the manufacturing organization; the distribution organization; and, finally, the sales organization.

CFO: FROM FINANCIAL MANAGEMENT TO STRATEGIC MANAGEMENT

Increasingly, expectations for the CFO are changing dramatically. Chief financial officer and their organizations are no longer seen as, and can no longer behave as, simple bean counters and scorekeepers. The CFO for the twenty-first century must be a provider of strategic analysis and appropriate measures, the source of *relevant* information and controls, and the keeper of effective and efficient process and transaction systems. In the rapidly changing business environment of today, a CFO who is slave to weak financial and operational systems and nonintegrated processes will not have a controlled business.

Leading CFOs are increasingly seen as true business partners within the executive team, providing increased analytical support and an enhanced understanding of all of the business's myriad processes, while at the same time seeking financial cost containment. SAP's software, because of its tight integration of information coming from throughout the business processes, can help cement the connection between the financial organization and the rest of the business. At the same time, however, implementation of the software causes changes to the CFO's organization.

Chief financial officers who view themselves and their staffs as technicians will be made obsolete by the software, which performs many of the routine tasks now done by people. Those who view themselves as business managers and who run a staff with holistic business skills, however, will find that the software helps them immensely, freeing them up from the day-to-day bookkeeping work and giving them more time to perform value-adding business analysis and business partnering.

Exhibit 3.1 shows the themes CFOs are being asked to examine in the area of developing true business partnerships and being the focal point for organizational integration throughout the business.

Henry Schacht, Chairman of Lucent Technologies, used the analogy of hockey when speaking to the leadership of his financial organization. Schacht spoke to them of Wayne Gretsky's comments that he does not look to see where the puck is, but rather where it will be going, so he can get there. Larry Byrd had the same kind of anticipation in basketball. The "long-bomb" football pass is predicated on the notion that the quarterback throws to a spot and the receiver gets there, both with an understanding of how long it will take the ball to arrive.

Schacht exhorted his financial managers to stop looking in the rearview mirror and start creating proactive analysis and measurements that can help their business partners in operations anticipate where the market will be, where the industry will be, and where the company will be

Exhibit 3.1   CFO Themes

in the future. "I don't want you to tell me what the numbers are, I want you to tell me what they mean," he concluded.

SAP software reduces the cost of financial record keeping from that entailed with current legacy systems. As corporations have grown through acquisition, and as business units have had the decentralized decision-making ability to purchase and use their own systems, some companies have created forests of competing and sometimes conflicting financial management software. In some instances, SAP R/3 software has replaced as many as 10 different legacy systems, providing a consistency of data never imagined.

This consistency of data allows for the creation of improved information for analysis. It provides a seamless reconciliation from the general ledger to subledgers and is updated in real time throughout the month—a must for companies that want to perform a "soft close."

Finally, it provides a basis for linking operational results and the financial affects of those results. A physical transaction cannot be booked without the resulting financial effect's being shown. This visibility of activities across finance and operations allows for a better understanding by operational managers of the effects their decisions have.

For instance, in one oil-drilling operation, a drilling engineer realized, after seeing the financial impact of his decisions in real time, that a particular chemical that was put down each hole drilled cost $150,000 per use. Using the chemical was just "the way things are done." After questioning himself as to whether there was really $150,000 worth of benefit to its use, he decided that there was not, and the activity was stopped.

In addition to freeing up the CFO's resources to become more of a business partner, SAP R/3 software helps CFOs and their organizations tackle the five other big issues facing the modern CFO:

1. Strategic issues, including strategic analysis and planning
2. Financing
3. Strategic performance measures
4. Strategic cost management
5. Processes and systems

Strategic Issues

The CFO is increasingly involved in strategic planning and strategic analysis for a number of companies. Among the emerging best practices in this area are a focus on competitive analysis; scenario analysis and best option modeling; end-to-end planning across the value chain from suppliers through customers, including lead competitors; and an emerging focus on both customer life cycle and profitability.

Exhibit 3.2 shows the business value chain and the variables that must be understood for customers, the company, and the competition.

Much of the information that goes into a company's plans is readily available—the state of the economy as a whole, customer perceptions of the company's products and services, and operational data regarding productivity and quality.

Competitive information is harder to get, but it can be obtained through published data, as well as the company's sales force, focus groups with potential customers, customer feedback, and supplier comments. Chief Financial Officers are increasingly being asked to create plans of action against customer performance benchmarks in the areas of working capital and resource productivity. Increasingly, companies compare their cost and

Exhibit 3.2   Business Value Chain Analysis

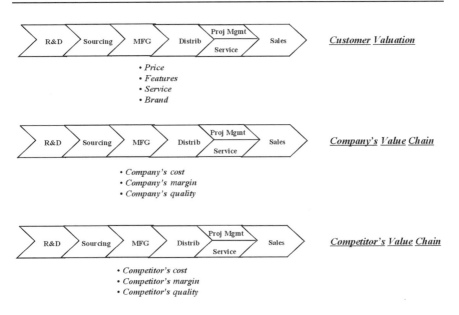

margin characteristics against their peers in the industry to determine if differences in capital or financial strategies offer a competitive window of opportunity.

The analysis of both internal information and competitor information allows a company to integrate strategic, operational, and capital planning. The availability of consistent internal data, integrated from operations to finance, provided by SAP software makes the job that much easier.

SAP software does not do "what if" calculations. If set up as an enterprise-wide solution, however, SAP software can be combined with strategic analysis software and used effectively as a data mine from which to pull relevant data for effective decision making.

Finance Issues

Exhibit 3.3 shows the main issues related to corporate finance with which CFOs are increasingly involved, including risk management, intergroup

Exhibit 3.3   CFO Issues

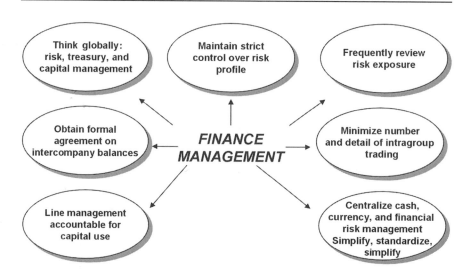

trading policies, and creating policies to hold line management account-able for capital use.

SAP R/3 software is helpful in this regard in a number of ways. Having an enterprise-wide view of assets allows one to maintain an enterprise-wide view of taxes and the effects of various capital allocation models on global taxation.

The software's treasury management module provides accounting information to support the treasury function, including foreign exchange, option pricing, derivatives, and other financial investments. This module ties in closely with a number of the specific industry solutions and also provides electronic data interchange (EDI) capabilities with banks.

One company using the software found that through rigorous analysis of the data available, it was able to reduce its worldwide tax burden by four percentage points, or $100 million a year.

Strategic Performance Measures

More and more companies are moving toward a "balanced scorecard" of measures. This transition from looking at purely financial measures acknowledges that if the physical (operational) aspects of the business are

Exhibit 3.4 New CFO Measures

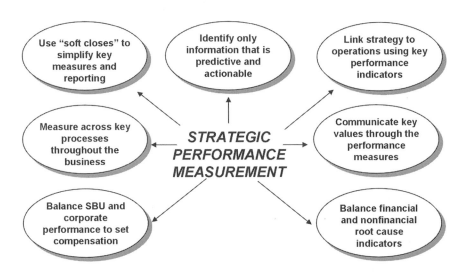

managed and measured well, the bottom-line financial results will be enhanced. Today's CFO is being asked to design strategic financial performance measures that are closely tied to the actual operational activities, rather than accounting measures that measure only arithmetic ratios.

Exhibit 3.4 shows some of the themes CFOs are increasingly examining when designing new measures.

The balanced scorecard approach truly comes to life with SAP software. With R/3, all of the data provided is driven by operations, and the proper linkages are made from physical operations to financial and accounting measures. The software is configured based on the physical flows; it automatically creates the accounting and financial details that will be captured around those physical flows. In that way, the management reports created from the data collected can be truly meaningful.

SAP software actually names activities and ties them together. The physical measures that are necessary to create an effective soft close are created, and what is actually driving the financial measures can be seen. Combining the company data derived from the SAP software with outside market data provides the ability to make forward projections for the industry and the company.

Properly implemented, the software allows the financial organization to support management by generating insights that describe and predict performance on a timely basis instead of merely describing history. The system accurately communicates to executives how the business is performing in the market and the degree to which further capital investment is warranted. It effectively encourages management to carry out the company's goals and maximizes the use of investment capital. It allows the company to anticipate and plan for fluctuations in key outputs such as revenue and operating income.

Strategic Cost Management

Chief Financial Officers are increasingly being asked to perform a number of different costing analyses across strategic dimensions, including the following:

- Product costing
- Activity costing
- Target costing
- Life cycle costing
- Customer or channel costing
- Project costing

Exhibit 3.5 shows a number of the tasks CFOs are being asked to undertake, while Exhibit 3.6 shows a flowchart of the kind of costing analysis the typical CFO is increasingly being asked to perform.

Many CFOs of manufacturing companies have become disenchanted with the old fully absorbed costing system based on labor costs. Manufacturing companies, especially those making high-tech products, are finding that their labor costs are only 5 to 10 percent of their cost basis, while materials account for 80 percent or more of the cost. They have scrapped the old standard costing system for a materials-only costing system, or a throughput costing approach that focuses on the reduction in the cost of materials. This allows companies to get close to actual costing.

Exhibit 3.5   CFO Activities

Because of this realization, companies are increasingly shifting to a simplified approach that permits financial costing to more effectively reflect the physical realities of the business.

SAP's R/3 software allows for improved costing information through a number of means. First, because physical activities are translated in a one-for-one manner with accounting entries, the software allows

Exhibit 3.6   Typical Cost Analysis

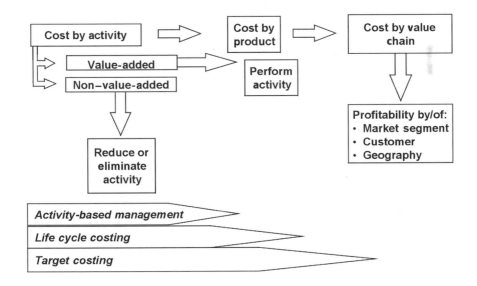

different focuses on the cost information to be created; one can "cut the pie" to easily look at customer, product, function, or process costs. There is also an activity-based costing module that allows activity-based management analyses to be performed. Because costing information can be derived from the general ledger, a number of different profitability analyses can be performed; committed costs as well as actual expenditures for a process or project can be examined.

Processes and Systems

Finally, the CFO is being asked to be the keeper of all financial processes and systems, and to play a major role in choosing, maintaining, and eventually discarding the technology that houses financial data.

Exhibit 3.7 shows the common themes about financial processes, systems, and technology that CFOs are asked to deal with.

A few of the most important themes are shared services for transaction information warehousing and enterprise resource planning (ERP) system support.

Leading-edge companies have come to realize that running multiple platforms or sets of financial transaction systems is not only not cost effective, but it is damaging to the company's ability to get required information on a timely and consistent basis. The financial transaction systems and processes are, with few exceptions, not core to the business. In order to run them most cost efficiently, most leading companies have already moved aggressively to develop shared-service centers in the United States. Lessons learned from these experiences are beginning to move to Europe and Asia, where cultural and other barriers have made the change more difficult.

Activities that are centralized in the shared-service environment are lower value-added activities that most business unit managers dislike having to perform. It is paradoxical that shared services is a decentralizing concept. By centralizing transaction-intensive activities in a shared-service environment, the decentralized business units can fully concentrate on the value-added business tasks they should be performing. This allows senior finance managers to fulfill their role as business partners.

SAP software facilitates a shared-service environment by providing a basis for integrated systems and eliminating legacy systems. The software

Exhibit 3.7   Financial Processes, Systems, and Technology

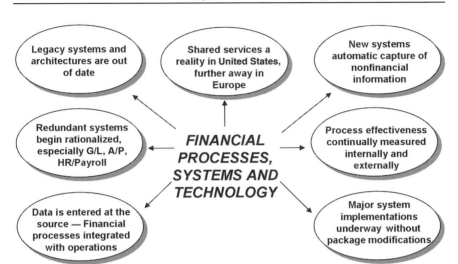

makes the transfer of information among applications easier. It provides an integrated basis for serving all business units from one base of information. It also facilitates reorganization of the business's systems. Under a shared-service model, supported by SAP software, the system infrastructure can be recoded rapidly. Many businesses have found that the system, when completely installed, increases their ability to change and reorganize.

SAP also facilities the development of a data warehouse, which is a common database, complete with standard and network interfaces, that allows for input of financial and operational information, output of management and financial reports, and answers to queries. Implementing a data warehouse requires augmenting the internal information template with data about key customers, employees, and process value drivers.

For companies with numerous systems, implementing a data warehouse means having to write translators from one system to another. Companies that use SAP have, within the software, the ability to create a data warehouse without any of the complex programming necessary for companies that rely on legacy systems. SAP software provides a consistent base on which a data warehouse can be established; the problems companies often encounter is in the interface between the various systems. SAP software establishes this interface and permits a consistent flow of information from the SAP system to the data warehouse.

HOW SAP SOFTWARE AFFECTS THE CFO AND THE FINANCE ORGANIZATION

When all is said and done, the proper implementation of SAP's R/3 software can facilitate removal of much of the accounting drudgery and many of the "bean-counting" aspects of a company's finance organization.

The positive side of this is that those within the transformed organization have more of an opportunity to become effective business partners, working with operational managers to build a more effective business.

The negative side is that many current employees within some finance organizations do not have the skills to be effective in the new organizational arena. A company will either have to put a lot of resources into retraining and upgrading skills or will need to find new employees with more high-level analytic skills.

4

How Will an SAP R/3 Implementation Affect Manufacturing, Distribution, and Sales Organizations?

MANUFACTURING ISSUES

The manufacturing organization has driven much of the change buffeting Western businesses for the last two decades. Management efforts in the areas of quality, just-in-time (JIT) delivery, business process re-engineering (BPR), and strategic cost management all have taken root in the manufacturing arena. The financial and information systems organizations have been dragged along, often kicking and screaming, into this frightening new world.

The goal of manufacturing is no longer to produce large, economically efficient lot sizes and production runs. In an increasingly automated manufacturing environment, labor costs are a smaller part of the picture; today, material costs are anywhere from 40 to 80 percent of manufacturing costs. Long production runs merely build inventory and use material, and give suppliers poor signals as to a company's critical material needs.

Manufacturing organizations are being driven to respond to the "voice of the customer" with new and innovative products, while maintaining low finished-goods inventory. There is an increased need for manufacturing flexibility, with smaller production runs and shorter delivery intervals. Long manufacturing runs do not allow a company to respond to more valuable customer orders because the planning has set the quantities. This crowds out customer opportunities.

The value chain in companies is already altering radically, and manufacturers are increasingly looking for ways to control the supply chain.

SAP software offers an enterprise solution that shows how operational causes equal financial effects by linking the operational systems to the financial and administrative support systems. The software enhances a company's ability to integrate operational information in real time, as well as order-status information in week, day, or real-time time frame.

The software provides a consistent set of product names in a central product registry; a consistent way of looking at customers and vendors; integration of sales and production information; and a way to calculate availability of product for sales and distribution, as well as materials management.

Integration of SAP modules enables better order-to-production planning; the sales and distribution module links in real time to materials management, production planning, and financials. This linkage of the company's physical activities to the financial impact of those activities allows for real-time profitability analysis.

It also allows for real-time visibility of customer orders and customer demand. Production planners can see what orders are in the pipeline and where they are, allowing them to plan against a near real-time forecast, based on actual orders. This could be done on a daily or weekly basis, reducing the production runs from the current monthly planning horizon that exists in many companies today. This permits better planning of build to order, build to stock, and a mix of order and stock.

The software allows modeling of anticipated orders. This can provide a probability that the sales opportunity will indeed turn into an order, based on past performance information. In addition, the moment an order is placed, the software can determine what unique materials are needed. This provides a company's suppliers with a vision of what its true needs will be, and allows time to secure critical materials.

Because financials are also tied to the sales, materials, and production modules, the "what-if" modeling capabilities also allow for forecasts to be based on actual or incurred costs. This allows the company to reflect current cost changes, and in turn provides a very useful basis for companies to move to a materials-only costing system.

SAP software's integration of sales and distribution with materials management and production planning allows stock to be adjusted instantly. Detailed materials resource plans can be created at least daily, but are available on demand. This, in turn, can (1) give suppliers more updated orders; (2) provide customers with an updated status of orders on a real-time basis and give them a perfected delivery date; and (3) maintain flow in processes, because no cutoffs are necessary to move information within the production planning and materials management cycle.

How SAP Software Affects the Manufacturing Organization

At the end of the day, SAP's R/3 software allows one to perform a number of simulations and modeling analyses and to:

- o See what shortages will be occurring
- o Expedite to eliminate the shortages
- o Obtain a better idea of when to order
- o Increase product line by 100 percent in a short time
- o See financial implications of each order, allowing orders to be ranked for margin and scheduled with priority for high-profit orders
- o Limit surprises to vendors
- o Link via electronic data interchange (EDI) with vendors for full JIT support through the supply chain
- o Provide vendors with more confidence in the company's orders

For nearly a decade, those who came to the business process redesign modus operandi from the manufacturing arena argued that BPR should not be driven by information technology (IT) systems, but rather by manufacturing and logistics. Information Technology, they argued, should be "enabling technology," assisting in the necessary process transformation. In truth, however, when they began making this argument, no off-the-shelf enabling technology existed to tie from the point of sales through manufacturing and distribution through the value chain.

For the most part, companies needed to build these enabling systems themselves, using a variety of packages. They could turn to early R/2 technology, which was still driven by a centralized mainframe architecture and therefore controlled by the information systems organization, with whom the manufacturing organization never really had the best of relations.

Today, enterprise resource planning (ERP) solution software provides that tool, and SAP's R/3 has the strongest manufacturing and logistics modules.

DISTRIBUTION AND LOGISTICS ISSUES

There are ten significant issues driving development of leading-edge strategies for logistics and supply-chain operations as businesses move toward the twenty-first century. They are shown in Exhibit 4.1.

Individually, each issue represents major change. Collectively, they redefine nearly all operational activities within companies, as well as the linkage to external trading partners. Traditional information systems support functional silos and are difficult to adapt to meet today's best practices.

Customer Franchise Management

Customer franchise management (CFM) is a fundamentally different view of how to think about and serve customers and leads to establishing customer-driven logistics and operations performance specifications. Exhibit 4.2 shows the major tenets of CFM. The major concept here is that customers are assets, to be enhanced over time by providing for their needs, delivering on commitments, and organizing the company's resources to meet customer needs.

Exhibit 4.1   Logistics and Supply Chain Driving Issues

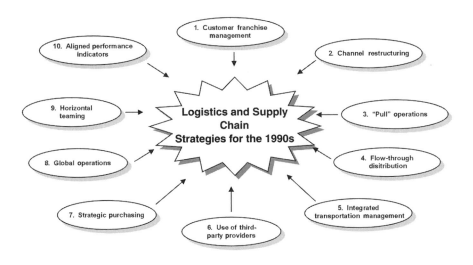

Exhibit 4.2   CFM Tenets

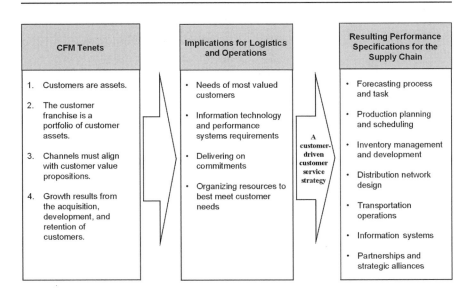

Exhibit 4.3   A $1.00 Baseline Consumer Goods Item Example

Trade Channel	Relative Price Point	Value Proposition		
		Value	Assortment	Convenience
C-Store	$1.60			✓
Independent grocer	$1.30		✓	✓
Drug chain	$1.25	✓	✓	✓
Grocery chain	$0.95 – $1.25	✓	✓	✓
Promotional/Mass merchant	$0.80 – $1.10	✓	✓	✓
EDLP mass merchant	$0.85	✓	✓	✓
Deep discount drug	$0.80 – $0.85	✓		
Club store	$0.75	✓		

Channel Restructuring

Channel restructuring seeks to optimize margins across channels. This requires understanding the cost/service tradeoffs of logistics options. Linked closely to customer franchise management, channel restructuring identifies the most cost-effective channel configuration that matches what the customer most values. This is seen in Exhibit 4.3.

Pull Operations

In a "pull" system, manufacturing and logistics operations are synchronized to more closely match the rate of actual product sales. Pull-based systems require a high level of integration across the supply chain.

Under the old push system, planning was manufacturing centric, and production was pushed to make product, even if this meant merely building inventory. Under the pull principle, customer demand is the driver.

Pull operations require a seamless, integrated IT support environment including state-of-the-art inventory management and forecasting tools, such as point-of-sale scanned data, Stock keeping unit-level (SKU)

Exhibit 4.4   Logistics Processes: Push and Pull

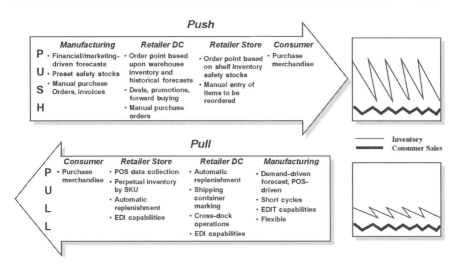

segmentation, dynamic forecasting, and automatic replenishment. The difference between the push and pull flow are seen in Exhibit 4.4.

Flow-Through Distribution

Flow-through distribution is necessary to support the pull concept. Distribution facilities must be transformed from storage to flow-through operations. This requires new processes, layout, and information technology. This difference in philosophy is seen in Exhibit 4.5.

Integrated Transportation Management

Integrated transportation management processes operate across the supply chain. Shippers are increasingly interested in establishing service requirements and then allowing a set of "core carriers/partners" to make decisions about low-cost modes and methods.

Use of third-party logistics providers across broader portions of the supply chain enables companies to concentrate on core competencies and reduce their asset base. Value-added alliances across the entire supply chain enables a company to do more with less. The change in decision

Exhibit 4.5   Old and New Distribution Philosophies

Old Philosophy	New Philosophy
Warehouse **"Manage the Storage and Handling of inventory"**	**Distribution Center** **"Manage the Flow of Product and Information**
Order Cycle = Months Weeks Days	**Order Cycle = Days Hours**
Inventory Turn = 1 5 10	**Inventory Turn = 12 26 52**
Characteristics • **Too many locations** • **Unfocused mission and role**	**Characteristics** • **Rationalized facility network** • **Focused mission**

process from traditional traffic management to logistics management are shown in Exhibit 4.6.

Strategic Purchasing

Strategic purchasing represents a significant leverage opportunity. Between 40 and 80 percent of the price of a manufactured good is the cost of materials, with high-tech manufacturers often spending only 10 percent on labor. Companies are increasingly switching to "materials-only" costing because labor, the traditional basis for standard costing, is no longer relevant. Companies are looking at benchmarking, re-engineering purchasing processes, and creating more tightly integrated supplier relationships.

SAP R/3 software, with its tight integration of modules, allows one to reconcile financial measures with operational measures more closely than ever before, and enables moving to a materials-only costing system.

Exhibit 4.6   Supply Chain Decision Process Change

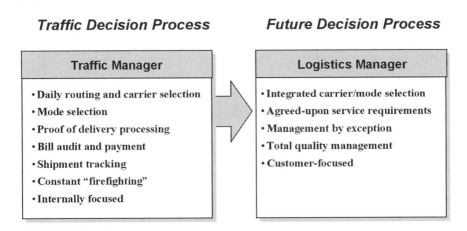

Traffic Decision Process **Future Decision Process**

Traffic Manager
• Daily routing and carrier selection
• Mode selection
• Proof of delivery processing
• Bill audit and payment
• Shipment tracking
• Constant "firefighting"
• Internally focused

Logistics Manager
• Integrated carrier/mode selection
• Agreed-upon service requirements
• Management by exception
• Total quality management
• Customer-focused

Globalization

Globalization of the supply chain will continue as companies seek improved sourcing and production options, and new market opportunities. With extended supply chains, the cost and service penalties of weak links, poor communications, and disjointed planning are amplified.

The enterprise that successfully evolves to a process-oriented organization, with significant horizontal teaming, will be best positioned to support profitable growth through its nonparochial, customer-centered culture.

Aligned Performance Measures

Finally, aligned performance indicators, rather than traditional indicators that measure functional silos, support customer-driven, low-cost operations. Companies in this new environment must realign their performance measures to highlight the key control points in the new manufacturing and distribution environment.

SAP software is an information tool that supports the kinds of cross-functional, process-driven, customer-focused logistics and distribution necessary in today's environment.

How SAP Software Affects the Logistics and Distribution Organization

With SAP's R/3 software, distribution can be more tightly integrated with manufacturing, sales, and financial reporting because of the tight integration of the software modules. This allows for integration of reporting *future performance indicators*, not just past performance measures.

SAP software enables real-time integrated forecasting of production planning and scheduling. It permits real-time ability to promise customer delivery dates. It provides an EDI linkage through the value chain to suppliers and distributors.

The software provides an integrated basis for managing the pull signals necessary to support the new distribution environment. Through EDI or new Internet interfaces, the software effectively supports the needs of global sourcing. It also provides a real-time, actual-cost basis to support material-only costing.

Finally, SAP R/3 software provides a financial analytic platform to determine the financial tradeoffs inherent in any logistics options, and provides a basis to support the new key performance indicators in this environment.

SALES ISSUES

All of the rivers of trends that course through businesses today can be traced to a single source point—the drive to satisfy and indeed delight each customer. That is because today's business finds itself in a true buyer's market.

No longer is there a market for every item every producer can make. Today's customers have an increasingly diverse array of choices across the product universe with which to satisfy their needs and desires. Companies fight bitterly for market share.

Markets are increasingly segmented, and high-tech database marketing is being utilized more all the time. Selling over the Internet is in its infancy. Point-of-sale data collection is becoming an ever more useful way to market and to understand in detail true customer demand. Companies are using that data to maintain their inventory by SKU.

Customer life-cycle costing analysis is just beginning to be used but will become a more widely utilized tool in the near future.

All of these sales efforts depend on the best data possible—data that links all phases of operations.

How SAP Software Affects the Sales Organization

SAP R/3 software enhances the sales environment in a number of ways.

Profitability Analysis. From a sales perspective, SAP R/3's main strength is profitability analysis [found in the controlling-profitability analysis (CO-PA) module]. Profitability analysis shows profits and contribution margins by segment of the company's business. These segments, properly called profitability segments, are customized to represent the company's view of its market.

A profitability segment could represent any combination of products, customers, sales channels, or other components. Profitability analysis uses integrated, real-time data for costs, revenue, and sales deductions, and also has planning and "what if" analysis capabilities. This will address the needs companies have always had for analysis of product profitability, geographic profitability, and the new measure of customer life-cycle profitability.

Pricing. SAP R/3 has functionality to handle very complex pricing scenarios. It is possible to design sophisticated pricing procedures that include numerous prices, discounts, rebates, and tax considerations. Accruals and statistical pricing elements can also be included. SAP's integration of data also enables prices to be determined based on a calculation of the product's standard cost. All of these pricing elements can be maintained by any combination of customer, customer group, material, material group, sales channel, or any number of other specified criteria.

Inventory by SKU. In the software's current release, there is no fully developed functionality for tracking inventory by SKU. There is a field on the material master in which a European Article Numbering/Universal

Product Code (EAN/UPC) can be entered. Custom reports could potentially be created using advanced business application programming (ABAP) to track inventory using this field rather than the standard SAP material number.

SAP is in the process of developing a bar-code scanner interface. It is likely that functionality will be developed in conjunction with this interface to enable inventory tracking by SKU.

Internet Capabilities. SAP is making progress on Internet selling. Electronic data interchange functionality has been available in the software for some time, and the company is extending that functionality to the Internet.

General Marketing. SAP software is currently not very strong in its general marketing information capabilities. This may be changing with the next software release. Also, within specific industry solution modules, the company is making progress in this area.

SAP is positioning its support of database marketing with its business information workbench (BIW). This promises a database to support business process redesign and the data associated with it. This will become even more useful as BIW is integrated into SAP's industry solutions such as telecoms and utilities.

Customer Commitment. SAP software provides an opportunity for the sales organization to project much more accurate delivery dates for orders. The software allows sales personnel to look into the company's finished-goods and work-in-process inventories, as well as materials availability to determine how quickly orders can be fulfilled. Since SAP software operates on a real-time capability, it can simulate availability of product on a monthly, weekly, or daily basis, if needed.

5

Are We Ready to Implement SAP R/3?

At this point, your company's executive management has developed a business strategy and an information technology (IT) strategy that are aligned and has determined that an Enterprise Resource Planning (ERP) solution is desirable. The choice has been made to purchase SAP's R/3 software.

You and your colleagues have begun to determine the scope of the installation program. You have gained an understanding of the business process change that will necessarily accompany that installation, as well as the areas of the business that will be affected and the degree to which they will be affected by both the software installation and the process changes.

Emotionally, you and the rest of the company's leadership feel that you are ready. Now you have to ask four tough questions about the company's readiness:

1. Do we have the capabilities—people with the business and technical ability to carry the program forward?
2. Do we have the financial resources to do it right?

3. Do we have the time to do it right?

4. Do we have a strong organizational culture, one that will be able to withstand the turmoil that is inevitable in such a large change effort?

If the answer to any one of these questions is "no," you can't really go any further. To change a "no" answer to a "yes" can be easy or difficult.

For question 1, capabilities can always be bought or, more realistically, rented in the form of consulting assistance or short-term employment of people with expertise.

For question 2, getting the financial resources is a matter of making this effort an executive priority.

For question 3, how much time is available may be a function of the reason the effort is being undertaken (discussed in Chapter 1), or it could be a matter of executive priority.

Question 4 is the really tricky one. If an organizational culture that can withstand radical change does not exist, a lot of organizational development work will need to be done. Some of this work must be done prior to beginning the actual implementation of an ERP solution, but much of it will be done coincidental to the ERP implementation.

COMMON MYTHS ABOUT SAP R/3 IMPLEMENTATIONS

Many corporate leaders gloss over these four questions. They do so because they fall into the trap of believing one of the four common myths about the implementation process for R/3.

Myth 1: I can hire all the SAP implementation resources necessary

You and 10,000 other companies will be chasing the same few hundred real experts. In today's marketplace, true SAP expertise has been bid up to phenomenal heights. Many SAP gurus have been captured by the big consulting firms, which can offer them better money than you can, as well as the prestige of being a consulting star and the ability to back away from programs that look as though the client is not going to carry them through the right way.

Myth 2: The entire implementation can be outsourced and not take the staff's time

It could be, but if you do this, you should count on turning over your systems to a third-party provider for eternity. SAP's software is so complex that if your people are not in the trenches working with it from the get-go, they will never get up to speed. Nobody in your organization will know how to run the software, maintain it, or upgrade it over time.

Given that buying the skills is not feasible and outsourcing the entire effort is politically untenable, you (and the head of IT) might be tempted to puff out your chests and give in to Myth 3.

Myth 3: R/3 is just another systems project, so the information technology people can do it themselves

You couldn't be more wrong. Enterprise resource planning projects are much broader and deeper than any systems implementation your company has ever contemplated. They are nothing like old-fashioned systems projects. The skill set necessary to carry them out are probably not there in your IT organization, which is why you considered Myth 1 and Myth 2 in the first place.

Now that you have accepted that the three most logical solutions—hire skills, outsource, and use only what you have—are all unacceptable, you come to the conclusion that the only way to tackle the all-encompassing nature of such an installation is to create a team of your best and brightest from both the business side and the IT side, and hire some temporary talent that has previously been involved with SAP software installations.

As you interview this consulting or short-term permanent (one to three years on staff) talent, do not let them know that you believe in Myth 4, or they will find another place to work.

Myth 4: R/3 can be installed in 100 days, even in a $20 billion company

Remember what was said in Chapter 2 (Exhibit 2.4): Depending on the complexity of the business and the degree of business process change being contemplated, implementation can take anywhere from three months to four years.

GET REAL REGARDING RESOURCES

It is time now to get real about the level of resources necessary to undertake an SAP R/3 implementation. Exhibit 5.1 shows the relative level of resources necessary at each stage of the implementation. Resources mean people, time, and money, but mostly people. Throughout the rest of this chapter, resources and people will be seen as synonymous.

The dotted line that extends ad infinitum at the point of maximum resources shows that if a proper knowledge transfer is not conducted to a company's permanent staff—from either hired consultants or short-term permanent expertise brought on board—the company will be in continuous "project" mode. Only when knowledge and expertise are successfully

Exhibit 5.1   Resources for the Implementation

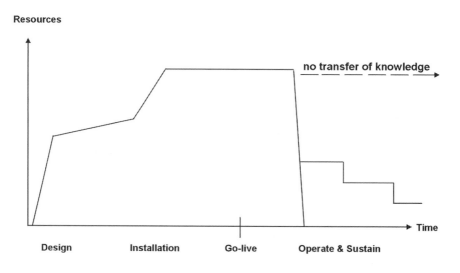

transferred to the company's personnel can the level of resources the company needs devoted solely to the SAP R/3 program be decreased.

We have deliberately put no numbers on the "resource" axis of Exhibit 5.1. That is because the number of people the company must put on the program depends on three variables:

1. **The degree of business change the company envisions incorporating into its implementation.** Thinking back to Exhibit 2.3, remember that we talked about the possibility of incremental business process improvement, which we define as moderate change, then in ascending order of more comprehensive change, there is business process reengineering, business process redesign, and business scope redefinition.

2. **The complexity of the business.** Exhibit 5.2 defines the various levels of business complexity. It is important to note that medium complexity means either multiple products and a national market or a single product with a global market.

3. **The scope of the program.** Typically, companies include the financials, sales and distribution, and manufacturing (which we lump together as logistics) in their scope. Many also add other business functions, such as human resources.

Exhibit 5.2   Definitions of Business Complexity

Degree of Business Complexity	_High_	_Medium_		_Low_
Product Portfolio	Many products	Many products	Single product	Single product
Vertical /Horizontal Integration	Vertically and/or horizontally integrated	Vertically and/or horizontally integrated	No integration	No integration
			OR	
Business Units	Multiple BUs	Multiple BUs	Effectively single BU	Effectively single BU
Operations	Domestic and International	Domestic only	Domestic and International	Domestic only

Exhibit 5.3   Project Team Sizes

Degree of Business Change	Complexity of Business	Scope	Team Size	Full Scope Team Size
Zone 1	Low	Financials	10	
		Logistics	12	
		HR	8	30
	Medium	Financials	15	
		Logistics	18	
		HR	12	45
	High	Financials	20	
		Logistics	24	
		HR	16	60
Zone 2	Low	Financials	20	
		Logistics	24	
		HR	16	60
	Medium	Financials	30	
		Logistics	36	
		HR	24	90
	High	Financials	40	
		Logistics	48	
		HR	32	120
Zone 3	Low	Financials	60	
		Logistics	72	
		HR	48	180
	Medium	Financials	90	
		Logistics	108	
		HR	72	270
	High	Financials	120	
		Logistics	144	
		HR	96	360

Exhibit 5.3 illustrates our suggestion for the size of the various project teams, given these three variables. Our numbers assume concurrent implementation, not sequential implementation.

For example, if you are a company with a medium degree of business complexity—a multiproduct organization with a national marketplace, say, working in zone 3—high degree of business process change—you would need about 270 people to do a full implementation of R/3.

However, if you are a company with a high degree of business complexity—multiple products and an international marketplace, but working in zone 2—a more moderate degree of business process change—you would need about 120 people to do a full implementation of R/3.

The message is simple. SAP designs its software to deal with any degree of business complexity, so it does not take all that many more people to implement the software for any degree of business complexity. It is the degree of business process change desired or required that makes the implementation a more difficult undertaking, requiring more people. To flip the equation around, the more people involved, the more complex the task of program and project management, which will be discussed later.

In addition, the ratio of people with expertise to those with no expertise in SAP should run about one for every three or four. That means that for a highly complex, zone 2 company, there should be about 30 people with SAP expertise for 90 without. Because recruiting and hiring 30 SAP mavens is a big chore, more often than not that means 30 consultants to 90 people from inside the company. Even those 30 consultants will have varying degrees of expertise, so it's important to negotiate strongly with the consulting firm to get at least some of its A-level players involved in the program to provide the level of expertise the company really needs.

CAN WE DO IT OURSELVES?

The answer is an emphatic, "Probably not." SAP software should carry a warning similar to a superhero's cape: "Use only under supervision; this does not provide you the ability to fly off the top of your office building."

We say this because the resource profile of an SAP R/3 implementation has a number of peculiarities. First, a much higher level of resources is typically needed during the design and installation than after the system goes "live." In addition, a number of the key skills required during the time of intense resource needs are skills your organization probably doesn't have, and for which there is no long-term requirement after the system goes live. If people are hired especially for the project, there may not be any appropriate role for them in the company after the system goes live.

This will mean hiring SAP mavens, at a premium, for a duration of 6 to 18 or maybe 24 months, then letting them go. These people may have no commitment to the company, only to their own advancement. If the project begins to drag, they may jump to another company that makes a better offer, unless you have locked them in. Most important, they may not have the communication skills and personality to fully transfer knowledge to those within your organization who will be responsible for maintaining the system after they are gone.

For this reason, most organizations utilize outside consulting assistance during an SAP R/3 implementation. The virtue of a consulting firm over a group of freelance "SAPnicks" is that the consulting firm works on a "client relationship" basis, meaning that although they are outside the realm of your organization, they still look to your success above their own. In fact, if you don't succeed, they don't, since the business world knows which companies are having a difficult time with their implementations and which consultants they are using. (Different consulting styles are discussed in detail in Chapter 13.)

Just because you're hiring a lot of outside assistance does not mean that you are not "doing it on your own." In a real way, an SAP installation is not something you can have done for you, or done to you. You must *use your outside consultants to your advantage.* That mean creating a strong internal program team, with strong program management, and strong project management of each project. Your internal people should drive the effort and manage the consultants, rather than the other way around.

COMPANY PERSONNEL ARE THE KEY

This means putting some of the company's best people on the installation effort; sucking the consultants dry of all of their knowledge and savvy about the software and the implementation process; transferring that knowledge into the organization through your people; and finally using your people to validate all they have learned, buff it up in the context of your corporate culture, and finally instill it into every fiber of the organization.

In order to do this, the implementation effort needs two different kinds of people from your organization.

First, you need business people. They need experience in the operational areas of the business that will undergo the most rigorous change. They should have broad-based experience in a number of areas of the company and understand the interactions between these areas. If your company has been through business process re-engineering or business process redesign, some of the people who were deeply involved in those change efforts should also be involved here. If you can find some "business" people with previous systems implementation experience, you are that much ahead of the game.

Second, these people must be strong team players and strong communicators. They must know how to explain and express what the business does and how it does it. They must be able to boil down the nitty gritty of any function into key points that they can communicate to the right people at the right time. They must also be tactful and diplomatic. This is going to be a long undertaking, and a lot of mistakes will be made. Finding mistakes quickly, and learning from them so that they are not made again is critical, and this must be done in an atmosphere full of motivation and free of recrimination.

Third, you need seasoned IT professionals. These people, like those from the business side, must be team players with good interpersonal skills—no geeks for this endeavor. The more systems project and implementation experience you can find, the better. The team must be made up of systems development people and "business analysis" people—those who understand the business and how it affects IT—rather than people who work merely as computer systems operators. It should have folks who have worked in a client–server environment as well as those who have worked in a centralized mainframe environment. Ideally, there will be some people who have worked in both environments.

As much as possible, it should have people with strong business skills. This is easier to accomplish now than in the past. Many companies now incorporate time within other functions and within business units into their IT management training, and today's true IT professional is a more rounded individual than those in the field 20 years ago. This may mean turning to some younger IT staff instead of those who have been around a long time; this issue must be handled sensitively.

Finally, if there is anyone in the IT organization who in a previous job had experience with SAP software, that person is key to the team. This experience may have been with another company or may have been with another business unit within the company that has already implemented SAP software.

PROGRAM AND PROJECT MANAGEMENT

It is important for an organization to have both program and project management, even if one of the selling points of the outside consultant you hire is its project management skills.

Consultants see the effort in discreet terms as an implementation. A company's program manager and project managers need to see the implementation as a piece of an organic, ongoing business operation.

The program and project managers lend credibility to the effort with the company's senior management—it is not just "something the consultants are doing." They facilitate access for teams and for consultants to the right people and resources within the organization.

They perform a valuable quality control and quality assurance function on the work being done by the team and by the consultants. They have responsibility for making sure the system being designed and implemented is the appropriate system for the organization, not just the whiz-bang system that makes the consultants look good. In short, they keep the consultants under control.

Most important, they provide an inside chain of command so that senior management does not need to be involved on a day-to-day basis. They are the 3 Cs (command, communication, and control) from the effort to the executive chain of command and back again. They also provide a point person for the staff who have been assigned to the effort, and are working in temporary, atypical, and highly stressful circumstances.

If the effort is small enough in scope, the project manager can provide mentoring and counseling to these individuals. If the scope is larger, the project manager can find the appropriate mentoring and counseling resources for an individual in need. Program managers, for their part, act as the same kind of resource for the project managers in larger and complex implementations.

What Kind of People Should Fill These Roles?

Program managers have to live at a high enough level of the organization where they have a network of high-level contacts and can break down barriers to the project's success. They must be the kind of people who can literally walk into any senior executive's office and say, "We have a brush fire, and we need x, y, and z resources to solve it, now, before it turns into a conflagration." The program manager is responsible for seeing the big picture, for managing the cracks between the discreet projects, and for making things happen across the organization.

This person may have been key in building a new plant, developing a new product, or market development for a product line. This person should have more than a passing understanding of contemporary information technology issues.

For example, one of the authors once worked with a person who could be a program manager for any business implementation effort. He was the program manager for construction of the airport in Saudi Arabia. He was not an engineer, a contractor, nor a financial analyst by training. His strength was his ability to understand sequencing, cost, and dependencies. He knew that the concrete for the easternmost runway could not get poured until the buildings on the eastern part of the airport had been constructed. He knew that electricians couldn't work until after plumbers had been in the first time.

In short, managing schedules, budgets, and human resources are the keys to program management. This means the need for someone who knows how to *communicate* effectively with those at all levels of the organization, as well as prime contractors and even subcontractors.

For the project manager(s), a person or people from the business side of the equation, not the IT side, are needed. Project managers will ideally come from one of the operational areas most heavily affected by that particular project within the overall implementation. They should have prior experience in project or program management for a large effort, not necessarily in the systems area.

Finally, if you can get someone with experience with a prior SAP implementation, all the better. This is usually difficult to do, since the person needs to be a long-time member of the organization to meet the other criteria. However, it is possible in companies that implement SAP on a business unit-by-business unit basis to get the project manager from the initial installation to then become the program manager as the effort is rolled out across three or four business units at a time, and to install people who were especially effective in the first implementation as project managers in each of the business units currently undergoing implementation.

This person should have some systems application experience, as well as experience *making things happen*.

WHY EXECUTIVE BUY-IN IS ESSENTIAL FOR PROJECT SUCCESS

Before your company can truly "start the engines" for an R/3 implementation, you must obtain buy-in from the entire senior executive team, and from the executives of all business units. For SAP to be truly worth the time, effort, and pain of the implementation process, your company needs to achieve true integration of its systems.

Without up-front buy-in, that integration won't happen. You will experience one or more of the following conditions:

- o Feuding among functional executives (operations vs. finance vs. information systems vs. human resources vs. sales). Everyone will be trying to steer the program to optimize their efforts, with the consequence of global suboptimization and lack of integration.
- o Active subversion or terrorism aimed at the program or particular projects by those among the rank and file who don't get a clear message from their functional or business unit executive that he or she has bought in to the effort.
- o Narrowing of scope, as particular executives decide "not to play" midway through the effort. Having to pull back on scope after a fully integrated system has been designed is almost as bad as a scope that keeps expanding.
- o Failure by parts of the organization to accept the system after installation, when it is live, because they feel it was pushed down their throats by outsiders against the wishes of their senior executives.

Any or all of these lead to a reduction in the benefits the company achieves from the effort.

Buy-in across executive ranks must not be tacit, but rather explicit. Executives must continually communicate to those who work for them, from their managers to the rank and file, that they believe R/3 is good for the functional or business unit organization.

One way to achieve buy-in across the organization is through strong sponsorship by someone near the top of the organization. Sponsors should be people who command respect from their colleagues across the executive ranks. Strong sponsors, working diligently among their executive colleagues, can reduce resistance, facilitate decision making, and mobilize resources. They act as the gatekeeper for the program manager just as the program manager acts as a gatekeeper for the project managers. Sponsors insulate senior executives from the need to be involved in the day-to-day machinations of the implementation effort, but keeps them fully apprised of the effort.

10-POINT READINESS CHECKLIST

Assuming you have a business strategy and an IT strategy that are aligned, and assuming that part of that IT solution calls for SAP R/3 as your ERP solution, you should ensure that the following 10 items are in place prior to initiating the implementation:

1. Senior executive buy-in is achieved across the organization, and senior executives agree to positively communicate their buy-in to those who work for them.
2. Senior executives are confident that the company's culture is ready to absorb the stress from a massive change effort, involving both business process change and total systems change.
3. The project's scope is clearly defined, and mechanisms are in place to assess any suggested expansion of that scope and make a quick decision, so that the scope does not metastasize on its own.
4. A strong, senior project sponsor is in place. Program and project management has been identified, is available, and is willing.
5. The anticipated business benefits are quantified and articulated across the organization.
6. Understand and have available knowledge of existing systems.
7. Resources (the project teams) have been identified and are available and willing.
8. Funding needs have been assessed, funding levels have been agreed to, and funding has been appropriated.

Exhibit 5.4   Overall Readiness: It's a Go!

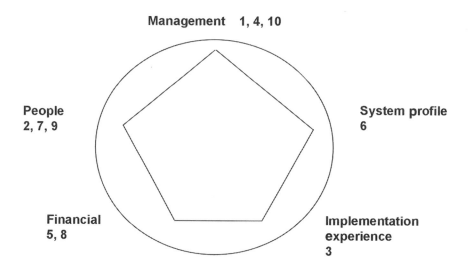

9. Consulting or short-term permanent staff needs have been identified, a decision on consulting vs. short-term permanent has
been made, and the source of that assistance has been identified
and hired.

10. Clear decision making and issue resolution mechanisms are in
place.

We have developed a "readiness pentagon" that shows how these
10 points line against five major headings. The pentagon is shown in Exhibit 5.4.

Exhibit 5.4 shows a state of overall readiness that points to "Go!"
The 10 points are well aligned, with appropriate levels of strength at each
corner of the pentagon. However, Exhibit 5.5 and 5.6 show situations in
which the organization's abilities are skewed so that it is imperative that
the organization think about whether it can proceed.

In both of these exhibits, we have skewed the organizational strength
in favor of system profile and implementation experience. This is by way
of showing that, in many instances, either by management design or by a
political process, ERP system implementation is seen as an information

Exhibit 5.5   Overall Readiness: Let's Think about It!

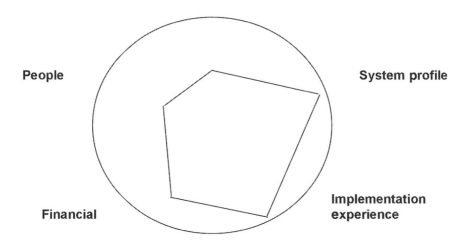

systems (IS) responsibility. Strength in IS is seen as paramount to getting the job done.

It is not. Without the proper financial, management, and people strengths throughout the organization, the potential ERP solution will turn out to be less than a solution for far less than the entire enterprise.

Exhibit 5.6   Overall Readiness: Let's Think about It!

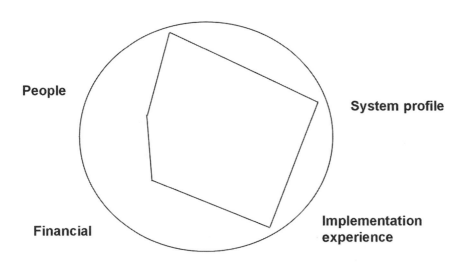

6

What Do I Need to Know About SAP R/3 Functionality?

SAP's R/3 software can be understood at its most basic level, or at its most complex. Most individuals in executive management do not feel it necessary to delve into the guts of R/3, but rather to understand it at a high level.

This chapter is for them. For those who would like to understand the software at a more detailed level, Chapter 15 provides an overview of the functionality in each of the major SAP modules.

The most important thing to understand is that R/3 is software that connects the entire enterprise by a logical transmission of data. When data becomes available at one point in the business, perhaps a sale, that piece of data courses its way through the software and the software automatically calculates the effects on other areas—need to manufacture a unit to replace the one sold, for instance, as well as need to invoice and perhaps open a new accounts receivable file.

This data is transformed into useful information by human manipulation, asking the software to create reports that collate data in a way that can be made intelligent. In this way, all of the collected data becomes information that can be used to support business decisions.

Exhibit 6.1   Overview of SAP

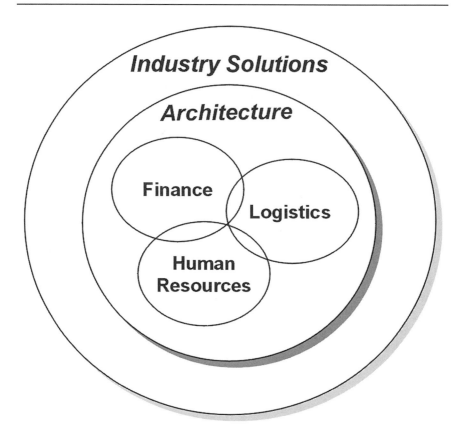

What is special about SAP's R/3 software is the degree to which all of the various modules are interconnected, and the degree to which each individual piece of data is made useful throughout the entire business system.

R/3 functionality can be broken down into five categories, each of which includes the following functional modules:

- Architecture
- Finance
- Logistics
- Human resources
- Industry solutions

Exhibit 6.2   Overview of SAP Modules

Architecture	Finance		Logistics		HR		Industry Solutions
Administration	FA	Financial Accounting	MM	Materials Management	PMGT	Personnel Management	Aerospace/Defense
BAP Developers Workbench	CO	Controlling	SD	Sales & Distribution	PD	Personnel Development	Automotive Chemicals Consumer Products
Business Engineering Workbench	AM	Asset Management	PP	Product & Planning	PA	Payroll Accounting	Engineering/ Construction Healthcare
Communications Workflow	TR	Treasury	PM	Plant Maintenance	OM	Organization Management	High-Tech/Electronics Oil and Gas Pharmaceuticals
	IM	Investment Management	QM	Quality Management	TM	Time Management	Public Sector Retail
	PS	Project System	SM	Service Management			Telecommunications/ Utilities

Exhibit 6.1 shows schematically how these five categories fit together.

Exhibit 6.2 shows an overview of the various modules within those categories that are available in R/3. Exhibit 6.3 shows the new functionality that is available in Release 4.0.

ARCHITECTURE

Exhibit 6.4 is a close-up schematic of the architecture category, showing the relationship between the modules.

The software's architecture forms the glue that holds the system's business applications together and provides the common business and technical functionality across the software. It includes what is called the "basis system" and system implementation tools.

R/3's basis system includes the data dictionary; system administration tools such as monitoring and security; tools for electronic data interchange (EDI), tools for allowing the system to work in a distributed hardware architecture, and programming tools for the advanced business application programming (ABAP) language.

Exhibit 6.3   Release 4.0: New Functionality

Architecture	Finance	Logistics	HR
Business engineer	Profit center consolidation	Available to Order	New countries, including:
Business information warehouse	Investment controlling	Web-based catalogues	Mexico (PMgt)
	Joint venture	Sales configuration engine	Taiwan (PMgt)
	Euro compliant	Flow manufacturing	Brazil (PA)
	Self audit	Sequencing	New Zealand (PA)
		Sample management	Employee self-service (ESS)
		Calibration inspection	Outsourcing interfaces

Exhibit 6.4   Architecture

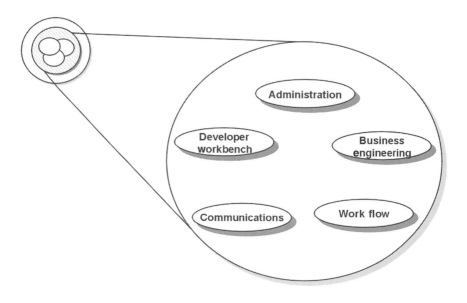

Also within the basis system are development and implementation tools and a guide to standard SAP business processes and configurations, as well as links to third-party tools. A more detailed discussion of these functions is found in Chapters 19 and 20. SAP has admitted that it cannot do all things for all customers and has partnered with a number of third-party providers to create tools.

Remember, SAP has defined its software around business processes, so it has defined the ways the business processes should be set up to use R/3 most effectively. That does not mean that R/3 cannot be configured to operate using the business processes as you have defined them or as you define them within any process re-engineering you do coincidental to implementing R/3. It is important for executives to understand the logic that drives SAP's business process definition; in some instances, you may want to let the software guide the way you define business processes.

FINANCE

Exhibit 6.5 shows a close up of the finance category and how the modules within it relate to one another.

Exhibit 6.5   Finance

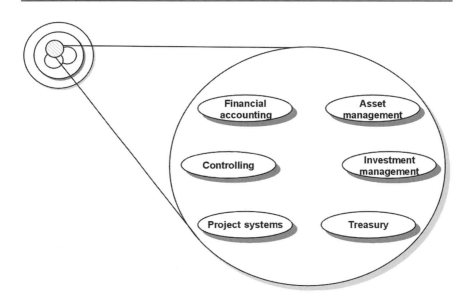

R/3's accounting area is a group of interconnected modules designed to meet both internal and external accounting requirements. The system reflects both the financial and management accounting effects of the business's operational events.

The way the modules are organized reflects a German accounting approach, befitting SAP's national origins. The traditional (U.S.) general ledger function is handled as a combination of the financial accounting (FI) module and the control (CO) module. These modules cover the functionality required for both external and statutory accounting (FI) and management accounting (CO).

Other modules are asset management (AM), capital investment management (IM), enterprise controlling (EC) and project system (PS).

All of the modules can be used in a multicurrency business. All are compliant with generally accepted accounting practices (GAAP) and leave audit trails.

LOGISTICS

SAP's definition of logistics includes both inbound and outbound transportation of materials and finished goods, as well as manufacturing.

Exhibit 6.6 shows a detailed view of the logistics category and how the modules within it relate to each other.

In the realm of logistics and manufacturing, R/3 provides integrated support for discreet, make-to-stock or make-to-order manufacturing. A number of "bolt-on" pieces of software from third parties are available to link computer-aided design (CAD) systems and mobile data entry.

Logistics modules include materials management (MM), production planning (PP), planned maintenance (PM), service management (SM), quality management (QM), and sales and distribution (SD), as well as the project system (PS) module, which is included as both a financial and as a logistics and manufacturing application.

As an example of the modules' functionality, go one level down into the materials management module, which is designed to optimize the purchasing processes using work flow, vendor evaluation, inventory, and warehouse management.

Exhibit 6.6   Logistics

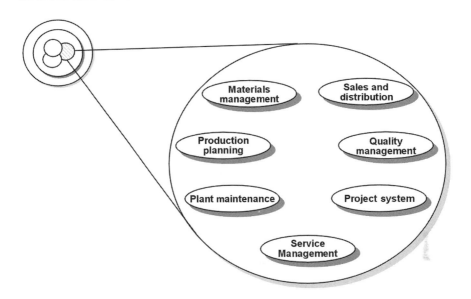

Major subdivisions of the materials management module are materials requirements planning (MM-MRP), purchasing (MM-PUR), inventory management (MM-IM), warehouse management (MM-WM), invoice verification (MM-IV), information systems (MM-IS), and electronic data interchange (MM-EDI).

HUMAN RESOURCES

Exhibit 6.7 shows a detailed view of the human resources category and how the modules within the module relate to each other.

There are five human resource modules: (1) personal development (HR-PD), (2) personnel management (HR-PM), (3) personnel administration (HR-PA), (4) organizational management (HR-OM), and (5) time management (HR-TM).

Within HR-PA are all aspects of employee management, including costs of recruiting and hiring, payroll, benefits, and travel and expenses. R/3 is able to handle national-specific human resource processes.

Exhibit 6.7   Human Resources

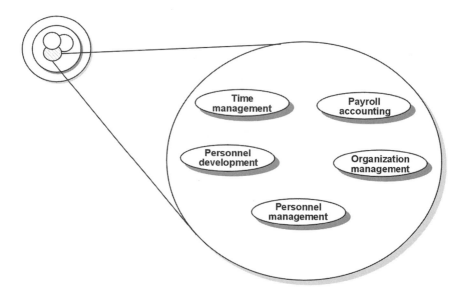

The HR-PD module includes personnel planning, seminar and convention planning, and workforce planning.

INDUSTRY SPECIFIC

Exhibit 6.8 shows the industry-specific module and all of the templates available within it.

Industry solutions are enhancements to the standard system. They address key issues within an industry and are often developed in conjunction with customers or consulting partners.

SAP and its partners have developed specific industry solutions for the following industries:

- o Aerospace and defense
- o Automotive
- o Chemicals
- o Consumer products
- o Engineering and construction

Exhibit 6.8   Industry Solutions

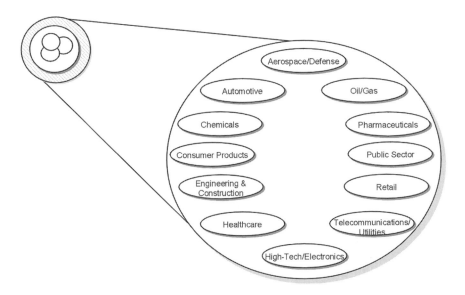

- o Health care
- o High technology and electronics
- o Oil and gas
- o Pharmaceuticals
- o Public sector
- o Retail
- o Software
- o Telecommunications
- o Utilities

7

What Will the R/3 Implementation Entail? An Executive Overview

The R/3 implementation will entail cost to an organization in time, money, and human effort. How much time and money are involved is directly affected by how much human effort you are willing to put into the implementation personally, and how much human effort you ask of the executive management team, the project manager you put in place, and the teams that are built to undertake the implementation tasks.

Make no mistake, installing SAP's R/3 and implementing the new business processes necessary to get the most from the software is nothing short of a major organizational change effort. In a major organizational change effort, nothing can substitute for sponsorship from corporate leadership. If you and the rest of the leadership team aren't behind it, no one else will be.

The following are the key tools and techniques necessary for successful implementation (See also Exhibit 7.1):

- o Risk management (see Chapter 13)
- o Project management (see Chapter 14)

Exhibit 7.1   Key Tools and Techniques

Risk management	Project management	
Change management	Process redesign	SAP methodology

- Change management (see Chapter 15)
- Process redesign (see Chapter 12)
- Methodologies (see Chapter 10)

A chapter will be devoted later to each of these topics, going into enough detail to assist project managers in carrying out their job.

Within the methodology we use, there are a number of discreet implementation steps. These are also described in greater detail later in Chapters 17 through 20, aimed at the implementor. In this chapter, the tools and the implementation process steps will be discussed briefly.

RISK MANAGEMENT

While it is impossible to totally eliminate risk from any business undertaking, it is possible to manage risk in a way that allows a business to take the most advantage of opportunities as they present themselves.

Our definition of a risk is *any factor that can affect the ability of the project to deliver results that are on time and on budget, at the expected level of quality.*

There are a number of different types of risk, as shown in Exhibit 7.2. There are organizational risks—the uncertainties that come about when undergoing any kind of change. These are mostly related to an organizational reluctance to change. There are also technical risks within the SAP R/3 software related to release upgrades, fixes, bugs, and so on. Any hardware purchased to make a system more effective carries risk inherent in its physical components. Any consulting purchased to assist with the hardware and software installation and implementation of business processes contains risk in its human elements.

Risk management is the sum of the actions that project managers undertake to mitigate all elements of risk inherent in a project. It is a

Exhibit 7.2   Types of Risk

	EXECUTIVE	
	PROJECT MANAGEMENT	
	TECHNICAL	
	ORGANIZATION	
	DECISION MAKING	
	FUNCTIONAL	

proactive process that reduces uncertainty and increases the likelihood of success.

Risk management must be part of the software installation and implementation process from the start. Risk management is easily overlooked as an extra use of time, money, and personpower. Poor risk management at the beginning of the undertaking can be seen as the cause of most SAP R/3 installation "failures."

A dollar spent up front on risk management can return dividends many fold in terms of time, money, and human effort saved as the installation moves forward.

PROGRAM AND PROJECT MANAGEMENT

Successful R/3 implementation demands excellent project management. R/3 projects are complex both technically and organizationally. They are large and wide in scope, often affecting individuals in every area of the business.

The software forces the business to begin operating with a process focus. An experienced project manager reinforces this, and is able to break through some of the functional silos.

Exhibit 7.3   Project Manager Characteristics

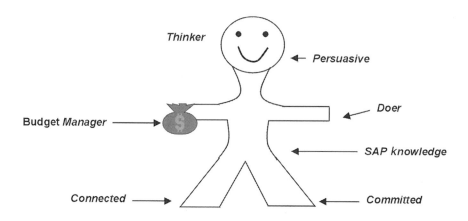

A good R/3 implementation program manager does not have to be intimately knowledgeable about SAP and its products. It is more important for this person to be intimately knowledgeable about the business and the way it currently operates.

A good R/3 implementation project manager must have a more detailed understanding of R/3 software, with at least a working knowledge of the software's integration.

While a program manager has more responsibility for thinking about the big picture, a project manager is both a thinker and a doer, a self-assured leader, persuasive, empowered, and most of all well connected and respected within the organization (Exhibit 7.3).

While executive leaders must show sustained commitment to the undertaking, it is understood that they cannot give the R/3 installation their undivided attention. The project manager can and must. This can be reinforced with significant rewards tied to specific achievements.

A process called goal-directed project management (GDPM), also known as milestone management, breaks the project into discreet pieces, sets objective measures for success for each of those pieces, and then determines if a piece of the implementation has met the criteria for success before allowing the process to continue on toward the next goal.

Like all large projects, an R/3 implementation needs a project structure, planning, budgeting, scheduling, resource allocation, and monitoring and control. The project manager is responsible for all of these on a day-to-day basis, and for reporting to executive management or to a steering committee put in place to oversee the implementation effort.

CHANGE MANAGEMENT

Change management involves aligning the organization's people and culture with changes in business strategy, organizational structure, systems, and processes. An active change management approach helps make a systems implementation project successful through the following:

o Building people's understanding of and commitment to changes associated the implementation

o Aligning key organizational elements such as structure, roles, and skills, to support the desired change

o Enabling continuous improvement to sustain the change

In order for the R/3 implementation to be successful, the vision of what the business processes will look like, and how data will flow throughout the information systems, must be regularly communicated from executive leadership to departmental leadership and the implementation project team. From the implementation project team members (who take a process view) and departmental leadership (who understand how this vision for business processes and information flow will affect the individuals in their department), this can be communicated to every member of the organization, as seen in Exhibit 7.4.

A quality change management effort provides ownership of and commitment to change, an understanding of how organizational structure has been designed to enhance how work gets done, and improved capability to adapt to future change. It is important at the beginning of the implementation of SAP's R/3 that a thorough organizational assessment be performed to determine the organization's readiness for change. A number of organizational variables must be assessed.

o *Motivation* is a key factor for adoption of the new technology and software, and improvement of the current business processes.

Exhibit 7.4   Change Management

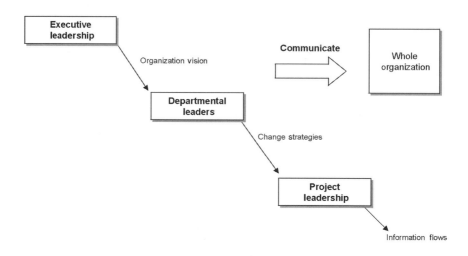

- ○ Individual *skills and abilities* must be matched with the task requirements of the implementation and the future state.
- ○ *Individual needs and values* must not be seen to be contradicted by the
  project. Areas of congruence can be highlighted to foster support.

Both *individual* and *organizational performance* must be monitored and
reported on. There must be clear mechanisms to do this throughout the
change process.

PROCESS REDESIGN

Implementing R/3 necessitates redesigning business processes that are affected by the data and information flow within the software. One of three
basic approaches to this task may be taken.

First, redesign from a clean sheet of paper—sometimes called "blue
sky" redesign. This is the technique our colleagues have often suggested in
their books on business process re-engineering.[1] When redesigning using
this method, one creates a *vision* of the utopian process and then designs to
get as close to that utopia as possible.

The upside to this approach, if done well, is that such redesigns can
lead to "breakpoints" where marketplace behavior can actually be changed

by giving the market something it never thought it could get from your industry until you "broke the rules" and set a new competitive target for all to shoot for.

Of course, the other side to this high potential reward is high risk; projects that shoot this high sometimes don't achieve their original goals.

It is important to recognize that one cannot do this kind of blue-sky redesign after undertaking the implementation of a major enterprise resource planning (ERP) solution. That is because the ERP software has some flexibility and can be tailed to a post–business process re-engineering (BPR) environment, but once the software is in place, making further major process redesign changes is very difficult. Sometimes, the choice of ERP software will be narrowed because of the way the company has previously redesigned processes.

Second, accept the SAP design. The information flow design within R/3 is predicated on an "ideal process design" as determined by SAP's software engineers, based on client experience and input. This ideal is often found to be less flexible than many organizations desire.

The upside to accepting SAP's ideal is that you can install the software much faster, not having to go through the "design" issues of process redesign yourself. This saves time, human energy, and money. SAP's accelerated SAP (ASAP) installation methodology for smaller and mid-sized companies ($250 to $2 billion in revenue) assumes that the company will accept the business processes as laid out by SAP. If a company does that, it may be possible to install the system in less than nine months, and in some cases in as little as 100 days.

On the downside is the lack of flexibility such an approach causes. The business processes as defined by SAP might not be appropriate for your industry. It can also lead to more complex data conversions from your current system, and possibly difficult interfaces because of data incompatibility.

Third, redesign with SAP in mind. This might be called using the SAP design as a default. It says, in effect, if the SAP definition of the process design gives 85 percent of ideal functionality, we will go for it. If the SAP defined process is less than 85 percent ideal, it is worth doing a custom design.

The upside of this approach is that it balances the time line and resource costs against reality. For most of the processes, you can use the plain

Exhibit 7.5   Process Design Approaches

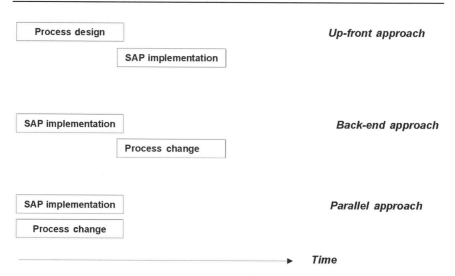

vanilla R/3 functionality and customize it only for the truly important processes that may be unique to your industry. It makes software upgrades fairly easy, and allows you to determine how much effort you want to put into data conversion.

On the downside is that you never get to 100 percent of your vision for business processes.

Our recommendation is usually to take the third approach. The path of least resistance is usually to meet SAP halfway and not to try to change the software to meet your vision, but rather to accept a speedy implementation of 85 to 90 percent of your vision and get on with the business of doing business.

There is enough flexibility within the R/3 software to meet almost all of everyone's needs. Installing the software galvanizes the need for process change, and process change overlaying a major systems implementation is traumatic enough for any organization. To back away from the systems implementation long enough to design business processes from scratch may simply overload the organization's capacity for change. Exhibit 7.5 illustrates various process design approaches.

The actual process redesign steps and time line will be discussed in greater detail in the chapters on implementation.

METHODOLOGIES

R/3 implementation methodologies are designed to be roadmaps for the implementation effort. All methodologies are structured and broken up into phases of work. They concentrate on breaking the effort into manageable and measurable work phases. In this way, milestones can be set and implementation progress measured against those milestones.

Some methodologies are sold off the shelf and can be used by a company implementing SAP or by a consulting firm assisting in the implementation. Other methodologies are proprietary and are sold by consulting firms as part of the consulting package.

SAP has created a methodology called ASAP, which works well for smaller companies with less complex business processes. For larger companies and those with more complex business processes, other methodologies are more useful.

Increasingly, those who partner with SAP and sell proprietary methodologies with their consulting are incorporating ASAP into their own methodologies for the sake of consistency.

Note

1. See Henry J. Johansson, Patrick McHugh, A. John Pendlebury, and William Wheeler, *Business Process Reengineering: Breakpoint Strategies for Market Dominance* (New York: John Wiley & Sons, 1993); and David K. Carr and Henry J. Johansson, *Best Practices in Reengineering: What Works and What Doesn't in the Reengineering Process* (New York, McGraw-Hill, 1995).

8

Competitors to SAP

It is important to put the term *competitors* into perspective.

In 1996, businesses worldwide spent about $70 billion to purchase software. Nearly $41 billion of that went to the top 10 software producers.

Of that $41 billion, about $6 billion was spent on Enterprise Resource Planning (ERP) solution software. Of that $6 billion, the top five ERP solution companies account for about 45 percent of the market. The other 55 percent of the market is held by about 40 other vendors.

SAP is ranked by market share as the largest vendor of ERP solutions. This calculation takes into account dollar volume, licenses, and installed base, but is a somewhat fuzzy number because each company licenses its products and counts customers in slightly different ways.

THE BIG FOUR

The discussion here will concentrate on the top four ERP solution providers, who are, in ascending order:

4. Baan
3. PeopleSoft
2. Oracle
1. SAP

Before the specifics of each of these players are discussed, a few common highlights should be noted.

First, these companies are all growing, either through acquisition or through internal growth. They are spending varying amounts on research and development (R&D), some preferring to buy new technology rather than develop it in house. They are all focusing new products on a distributed architecture model, with networks, distributed databases, and distributed applications.

Second, they are all being driven, to one degree or another, by technologies they cannot control, especially the Internet and World Wide Web.

Third, they are all being driven to some extent by Microsoft and its Windows NT front-end operating system, as well as its back-office server systems that use structured query language (SQL) technology.

Fourth, these companies are tacitly dividing the marketplace as they focus more heavily on targeted solutions for vertically integrated industries, such as health care, pharmaceuticals, automotive, public sector, or process manufacturing, to name just a few.

Fifth, all of the companies are compliant with the year 2000, meaning that their code is written in such a way as to acknowledge the new millennium. Old code is written to acknowledge only the last two digits.

Finally, they are all pushing to make their software capable of providing a truly integrated supply chain, allowing linkage from customer through operations, sales, and financial, and out to vendors.

We will look briefly now at who these four companies are and how they are focusing their strategy as we move toward the twenty-first century.

Baan

Founded	1978, Netherlands
1996 Worldwide software revenues	$268 million
1996 Revenue growth rate	103 percent
1996 Ranking, ERP software	4th
1996 ERP market share	±4.5 percent
1996 Ranking, total software	38th
Investment in R&D	11 percent of revenue

Baan provides an integrated family of manufacturing, distribution, finance, transportation, service, project management, and process modeling modules. The company is responding to changes in open technologies—Web and Internet—incredibly fast.

The company's strategy is growth through acquisition. Recent acquisitions include Antalys, which provides price and configuration products that link the sales channel with the manufacturing pipeline; and Berclain, which provides manufacturing synchronization and scheduling software. Baan also has developed joint ventures, most notably with Hyperion, the leader in finance, budgeting, and planning software.

Baan has cutting-edge, Web-enabling technology, and can provide work flow data over the Internet or an intranet. The company is moving to strengthen its product offerings in human resources and electronic commerce.

Baan is targeting aerospace and defense, automotive, electronics, heavy equipment, and contract manufacturing, as well as process industries. The company had its first big success in the United States when it signed Ford as a client.

Peoplesoft

Founded	1987, United States
1996 Worldwide software revenues	$389 million
1996 Revenue growth rate	88 percent
1996 Ranking, ERP software	3rd
1996 ERP market share	7.3 percent
1996 Ranking, total software	30th
Investment in R&D	16 percent of revenue

PeopleSoft is still thought of by many as a human resource package, although today it provides integrated modules in financials, material management, distribution, manufacturing, and human resources.

The company has traditionally sold its products in the U.S. market and is only now becoming a truly global player. Growth has been both through investment and sales, and by acquisition, especially the purchase of Red Pepper, a highly regarded provider of supply chain management software.

PeopleSoft is riding the open architecture wave very effectively, linking smoothly to provide Internet and Web-based transaction capabilities for its clients. The company's enterprise resource optimization (ERO) scheme seeks to allow clients to do real-time planning instead of batch planning, and it is incorporating artificial intelligence into its products, building a smart system for forecasting and demand planning.

The company is marketing heavily into higher education, health care, and the public sector at all levels of government, as well as manufacturing, financial services, and retail.

Oracle

Founded	1980, United States
1996 Worldwide software revenues	$3,615 million
1996 Revenue growth	38 percent
1996 Ranking, ERP software	2nd
1996 ERP Market share	8.9 percent
1996 Ranking, total software	5th
Investment in R&D	9 percent of revenue

Oracle's ERP product is second, behind SAP's. It provides 35 integrated modules that cover financials, human resources, manufacturing, distribution, project management, sales force automation, and supply chain management.

The company uses its position as a provider of database software effectively, increasing sales into companies that are using its database software on distributed systems by assuring companies of compatibility. Oracle seeks growth in what it calls the "virtual enterprise," integrating the supply chain through a combination of Internet-based architecture, a "thin client" at the front end, and robust distributed applications.

Oracle is focusing its efforts heavily in the consumer packaged goods (CPG) industry, as well as in energy, government, higher education, and pharmaceuticals. Finally, the company is concentrating on the environmental, health, and safety industry.

SAP

Founded	1972, Germany
1996 Worldwide software revenue	$1,692 million
1996 Revenue growth rate	25 percent
1996 Ranking, ERP software	1st
1996 ERP market share	28 percent
1996 Ranking, total software	7th
Investment in R&D	16 percent of revenue

SAP continues to have the most robust software. However, the company is bound to supporting a large, installed client base that is still using mainframe architecture for R/2 and early client–server R/3 technology. This means it is challenging for the company to respond to new trends and support new technologies.

Providers of third-party tools are assisting in this area, but the company must play a different role in relation to cutting-edge technology than that played by its major competitors. In addition, the company has always grown internally by developing new software products, rather than by acquisition, and so may be losing out on advancing its technology that way.

WHERE WILL THEY BE IN 2000?

That, of course, is the $64,000 question.

We predict that the industry will continue to consolidate and that, by the new century, the top four players in the ERP industry will probably control 65 to 75 percent of the market, if not more.

Baan is still a preferred provider for many manufacturing companies, and PeopleSoft is still perceived to be the strongest software package in terms of human resources capabilities. Oracle is still the natural candidate for those who seek the most simplicity. All are less expensive than SAP, but for those who want the safety of going with a tried and true provider, SAP will continue to be the company to deal with.

Increasingly, we are finding that companies are in a situation where products from two, three, or even four vendors are present in their various operating units, and that the real challenge is making those different products talk to one another. Some companies are doing this in a rational way, seeking "best of" packages for each business function, then tying them together. Others are doing it in a more haphazard way because of inability to reach consensus, or decentralization that allows operating units to choose system packages without any central coordination.

Those who spend their time primarily on SAP implementations are eagerly awaiting the release of R/3 Release 4.0 to see how the company deals with the issues of open architecture, the World Wide Web, and the Internet.

Part II

The Implementor's View:
Tools and Issues

In this part, we look at the implementation of SAP R/3 software not from the perspective of the executive suite, but rather through the eyes of those put in charge of day-to-day implementation. These implementors have a number of tools they can use to further their implementation goals, from working with consultants in a partnering relationship to predesigned methodologies that allow them to adopt and adapt best practices from others who have implemented before them.

Increasingly, they are provided with software tools and bolt-on packages that extend SAP R/3's functionality and make the implementation task run more smoothly and effectively.

At the same time, they must deal with a host of issues throughout the implementation process. The largest part of an implementation officer's task is to mitigate against the risks inherent in the implementation—organizational risks, technological risks, and business risks. This is accomplished by performing process re-engineering simultaneous to R/3 implementation, by rigorous program and project management, and by working diligently on the human relations side of equation (change management) to steer the organization through the implementation effort and into the company's future state.

9

Partnering for Success: Proceed with Care

SAP's R/3 software comes with an implicit warning:

Do not try this at home alone!

Very few, if any, companies without previous experience will have the capability to install, implement, and maintain SAP's R/3 software. Some do try to hire the capability in-house, but most companies turn to consultants to help them in an R/3 implementation.

SAP realized years ago that its strength lay in developing and marketing the software, not in helping clients implement it. Therefore, early on, SAP developed partnerships with a number of different consulting firms of various sizes and styles.

In turn, by seeking out the SAP consulting partner or partners that best fit its needs, a company can greatly increase its chances of a successful implementation, defined as on time, on budget, and providing the company with all the functionality deemed necessary.

This chapter will describe how one can truly manage the process of partnering with consultants—and how to manage the consultants themselves—in order to get the most from SAP's software.

WHY USE A CONSULTING PARTNER?

Installing, implementing, and maintaining SAP's R/3 software is a large, complex, and risky task. Turning to a consulting partner for help does not make the task any smaller or less complex, but it can greatly reduce the overall implementation risk.

Consultants have done it before and have seen both successes and failures in a number of different organizational contexts. You can learn from the mistakes of others by having consultants get you through the minefields that have damaged other companies, and transfer their knowledge of best practices to you.

Consultants understand the logic and integration behind SAP's software, and can expedite an organization's going up the learning curve without adding to its permanent payroll. They can help quicken the implementation cycle by focusing the company's decision making on the true issues. However, they can't quicken the implementation cycle if the company's leadership has difficulty making decisions.

Exhibit 9.1 shows the partnering relationship between you, SAP, and the consultant or consultants you choose to work with. This triangular partnership means that you, SAP, and the consultant or consultants you choose to work with all have a common goal—the success of your project.

TYPES OF CONSULTING PARTNERS

There are five types of consultants that work with SAP:

- o Big Six accounting and consulting firms
- o Hardware vendors
- o Boutique, or specialist, consultants
- o Body shops
- o Independents

In addition, SAP has recently created its own consulting organization, which is growing rapidly.

Exhibit 9.1   Partnering Relationships

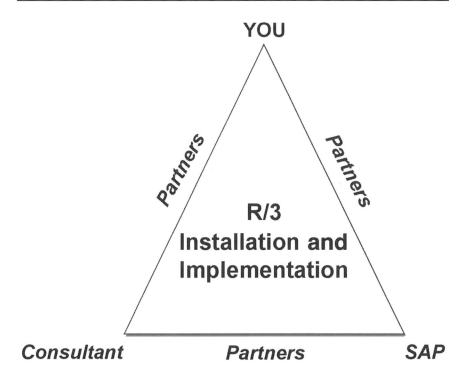

YOU

Partners   *Partners*

**R/3
Installation and
Implementation**

Consultant   *Partners*   *SAP*

The Big Six

All of the Big Six accounting and consulting firms have practices in SAP implementation. Practitioners at all of these firms (of which the authors' employer is one) look at SAP installation and implementation as a business issue, not merely a technical issue. They know about business process re-engineering (BPR) issues, as well as quality and change management. If they need help in these areas, they can turn to other practice areas within their firm. These firms are very strong on project management skills. They are also generally the most expensive.

Hardware Vendors

Hardware vendors such as IBM and Hewlett-Packard have increasingly set up consulting groups as a way to add value in after-sales service. They are very valuable for issues of network sizing and other hardware questions. They provide very strong technical expertise but little in the way of BPR, and they usually do not do much project management or project planning.

Boutiques

There is a growing number of small, specialized consulting firms growing up to solve particular issues surrounding an SAP implementation project. Some firms specialize in one tool, such as application link enabling (ALE). Others specialize in training, testing, or documentation. They can either be hired as subcontractors to your prime contractor, or you can hire them yourself. We would recommend contracting with them directly.

Body Shops and Independents

This is the old data processing consulting model. The consulting firm sends bodies, and you provide the management. Consultants from these kinds of firms do not take on much responsibility; rather, they do what they are told. You accept all the risk.

SAP'S CONSULTING PRESENCE

As SAP is marketing more heavily to small and mid-sized companies ($250 million to $2 billion), it is looking to provide consulting services for installation and implementation. SAP realizes that many of these companies can have a fast implementation if they are willing to use SAP's standard modules and definitions. In addition, these companies do not have the financial resources to hire Big Six consultants, but if they try to do it themselves or hire less-than-qualified consulting help, they run a very high risk of failure, which would look bad for SAP as it reaches into this enormous market.

SAP's consultants are a strong source of application and technical specialization. They are geared to the Accelerated SAP (ASAP) installation process, which does not work with large companies (or companies not willing to adopt "vanilla" SAP process definitions).

SAP is increasingly competing against the Big Six accounting and consulting firms for engagements with smaller and mid-sized companies, and winning on the basis of lower price. Currently, SAP has a new concept, "Team SAP," that targets work for larger clients directly. Generally, this addresses larger companies' complaints of SAP's lack of involvement in their projects.

Most consultants will welcome this involvement, as it "puts SAP's skin in the game." However, at this time, SAP is still weak in the areas of BPR and project management. Because of this, it is still important for larger companies to have a business-oriented consulting firm working alongside Team SAP in a large, complex implementation.

SEEK COUNSELING, NOT JUST CONSULTING OR IMPLEMENTATION

There are three kinds of consultants in the world: (1) implementors, (2) consultants, and (3) counselors.*

Implementors do the trench work. They are task oriented. Within any consulting project, there are a number of implementors working away. An SAP installation and implementation demands large numbers of implementors.

Consultants understand the business issues involved in a project. They are able to manage the implementors, spot problems, and discuss with you the various options for correcting problems. While they have a much higher level of business knowledge, they focus their interactions with you around the task at hand.

Counselors give advice about a broad range of business issues. These may or may not have to do with the current project. They will give you their best advice even if is not always to their advantage. They may tell you to hire another firm to do a particular consulting job. They do this based on the relationship they have with you, and with the knowledge that you will turn to them for their expertise and hire them when they believe they can do the job as well as or better than a competitor.

The best counseling often comes from the firm that does your company's auditing. Your auditing firm, especially if it is your long-time auditing firm, should have developed a network within your business. Complementing this with the network that any good consulting counselor has developed over the years, your audit firm should be able to provide you with good intelligence about what's going on both inside and outside your company as you undertake the SAP R/3 installation and implementation.

Another reason to look to your auditing firm as a natural consulting partner for your SAP R/3 project is that your auditor has a vested interest in a successful outcome. There is a relationship there and a desire to make SAP truly work for your business. Your auditor has a way to go right to the chief financial officer (CFO) if there is a problem. A word of caution here: Your chief information officer (CIO) may see this as a threat, though it need not be.

A strong consulting team should have within it at least one counselor, a handful of consultants, and numerous implementors.

USING MULTIPLE CONSULTANTS

Depending on the size of your company and the style with which you like to operate, using multiple consultant organizations is often a valuable approach. Some of this may be dictated by your company's policies, some by company politics. There is also some common sense to this approach.

Your company may have a policy that precludes your auditing firm from being the sole consultant on certain kinds of projects or on projects of a certain size. In this case, you may need to look for a direct competitor of your auditing firm among the Big Six to be the lead consultant. The project might be split into two large pieces, with an auditing firm hired for one piece and a competitor for the other.

There may be a need to hire two major consultants because of internal political squabbles between the CFO and the CIO. The CIO may feel uncomfortable having your auditing firm—with its close ties to the CFO—as the prime consultant on what he feels is an information technology (IT) project.

Having two Big Six firms support the process can be a way to keep each of them honest. However, when you are using two prime contractors, it is important to split the project at a logical place. If you do not, things can become chaotic. Also, more than two major players can lead to chaos.

The vendor of the hardware your company uses can probably provide some useful consulting help, regardless of who the prime consulting firm is. You may need the services of one or a few boutiques for some specialty work. Increasingly, SAP itself is turning into a useful member of your consulting team; SAP also has a vested interest in a successful outcome.

You probably will not want to ever use a body shop, unless you have made the decision to hire in senior-level SAP specialists, in effect hiring in your top level of consulting talent. If you do that, those individuals who are hired in as the project management may want to look for temporary staff to keep the payroll from getting bloated.

Regardless of who you hire as your consulting partner for the SAP installation and implementation, you want to look for a consultant who is going to engage in knowledge transfer. The consultant should work with your staff to help them learn some of the intricacies of R/3 and gain experience. There should be a heavy emphasis on training, with clear documentation and "training trainers" so that your company can continue to push knowledge of SAP throughout the organization.

KEY QUESTIONS TO ASK WHEN SELECTING A CONSULTANT

The major questions to ask when selecting a consulting partner fall into three categories: (1) staffing, (2) track record, and (3) fees.

Staffing

Be sure that the people who make the sales call and close the deal are going to be involved in the project. At the meeting when the deal is closed, the consulting partner should commit in writing to the project manager and some of the key staff people as to the percentage of time that will be devoted to your project. *Have this confirmed in writing!*

You do not want the project staffed totally by consultants who have just been through SAP's partner academy and are one step ahead of your own staff.

It is also important to find out if the staff needs to travel or if they are local. Travel adds cost, but sometimes you must pay extra to get the most experience. Try to strike a balance between cost and experience.

Finally, with regard to the staffing ratio, there should be one consulting staff person for every three to five staff members from your company. This ratio may fluctuate depending on the phase of the implementation, how many specialist consultants are necessary, and how many programmer consultants are necessary to write interfaces and other specialized code.

Track Record

A potential consulting partner should be able to provide at least a handful of quality references that can show success in terms of a project completed on time and within budget and providing the requisite functionality that was defined at the project's inception. At least some of those references should be from companies that are similar in size to yours and in the same industry.

Fees

Fees range widely among consultants for SAP projects. You will pay a premium for a Big Six firm, but it is usually worth it for the scope of services provided and the level of business acumen these firms bring to the project.

Watch out for firms that low-ball competitors on price, especially when they offer a fixed price for a small initial part of the project or for scoping the project. They may define the project's scope narrowly in order to keep their quoted price low, but when you get into the project you find that the scope inevitably widens. This happens very often in an SAP implementation, due to the degree of integration in the software.

In this case, you often end up with numerous costly change orders, and the "a la carte" price is often more than it would have been had the scope been defined properly in the first place. One of the most important tasks you will ask your consulting organization to do is to help you determine the proper scope of the implementation and create ways to keep the scope well defined throughout the effort.

Professional fees are charged (exclusive of expenses) on a daily or hourly basis. If hourly rates are proposed, be sure to cap the number of billable hours per day. Also, be sure to address travel time and overtime.

OTHER THINGS TO LOOK FOR IN THE CONSULTING RELATIONSHIP

The market for SAP R/3 consulting is growing so quickly and consulting firms are signing on to projects at such a rapid rate that some are having trouble finding enough qualified personnel to fulfill all of their engagements. Because of this, you may not be getting what you thought you were supposed to when you signed an agreement.

Bodies may be slow to appear at your site, and when they do, they may not be the people who appeared in the proposal. This can mean that those people have left for another job, or it can mean that they are jammed up on another assignment that is behind schedule. However, it may just be a bait and switch tactic, where the "platinum" named consultants in the proposal very rarely make an appearance at any client's site.

If platinum-type consultants are making frequent appearances at your site, when you did not think they would be there as often, it could mean that your consultant is staffing your project with a lot of "90-day wonders" who have only been through SAP's partnership academy. Many of these folks are only an hour ahead of your people.

GETTING THE MOST OUT OF CONSULTANTS

The key to getting the most out of consultants can be summed up in the following two sentences:

1. Manage them, do not let them manage you.
2. Remember who is paying whom.

It is important not to let consultants take over a project. When this happens, you lose the necessary "buy-in" from your organization.

It is just as important to treat consultants as equals with your own employees. That means you should not exploit them nor dump on them. Right now, it is a seller's market; consultants can pack up their bags and begin work with another client the next day.

While you should never exploit them as people, you should always exploit their knowledge. After all, you are paying for their experience, and you should never hesitate to solicit their input. They can let you know both what is going on in various parts of the project and what went on in past projects on which they have worked.

Consultants can play a very useful role in keeping your company politics honest. Someone from the consultant's organization should be placed on the steering committee.

Finally, the goal is to complete the project and get the consultants out. This allows them to move on to their next job and allows your company to get on with its true business, with SAP's R/3 in place, making your company's record keeping more efficient.

10

Methodologies

In an SAP R/3 implementation, it is usually helpful to follow a clear and well-defined methodology. A methodology is a structured approach to accomplishing a larger work effort.

An R/3 implementation is often the largest business change activity a company will ever undertake, although many companies do not realize this when they begin the effort. A methodology serves to break down the entire work effort into a series of steps that must take place, over time, in the proper sequence or in small groups of parallel steps. An R/3 implementation methodology tries to describe all possible steps necessary to implement the program.

Computer software methodologies have been around for close to 40 years. Beginning in the 1960s, common standards were developed for programmers to make development and maintenance of software easier. The 1970s brought a systems approach. During this time, hardware costs began to fall rapidly, and programming became less of an art and more like a manufacturing process. Companies shifted their computer-services focus from hardware to software to achieve maximum benefit.

The 1980s saw the advent of structured systems approaches. Business needs, and not just information technology (IT) needs, began to be considered. Object-oriented programming languages were born, and computer-aided software engineering (CASE) tools were developed. The focus was on an organization's data and functions. The goal of CASE was to automate the process of turning a business requirement into computer code.

Unfortunately, CASE as originally conceived was a flop, although there are some who argue that today's Enterprise Resource Planning (ERP) solutions are, in fact, CASE tools. In essence, custom computer software had become so complex and programmer intensive that it began to collapse under its own weight. The effort to develop custom software became so all consuming of resources (time, people, and cash) that companies began to hope and pray for a commercial package they could buy and modify.

It was into that world that SAP, Oracle, and the other producers of enterprise solution software were born. These companies provide ERP software that can be customized and that does not require CASE technology. The coincident emergence of business process re-engineering (BPR) led to the attempt to use ERP information technology as an enabler for process enhancement.

Today, enterprise engineering solutions allow businesses to forget about developing software and instead concentrate on developing business solutions utilizing packaged software. The only code that must be written is for conversions and interfaces with the legacy systems that will remain, and much of that work is being taken over by code-generating tools.

BENEFITS OF USING A METHODOLOGY WHEN IMPLEMENTING R/3

The first benefit of using a methodology is the risk reduction that comes from using a proven approach. Another benefit is the creation of a common framework for all teams to work with. This includes standard *terms* and the coordination of *time lines*.

It also provides a rough guide as the overall work effort that will be needed. This breakdown of *tasks* is very important for a smooth implementation.

Most methodologies include *templates* that show examples of normal project deliverables, which provide project teams with guidance for their detailed work.

Exhibit 10.1   Top 10 Risks to an SAP R/3 Project

---

1. **Inadequate sponsorship**

2. **Poor/slow decision making**

3. **Poor/no scope definition**

4. **Inadequate attention to change management**

5. **Lack of cooperation between business areas/departments**

6. **Poor use of consultants**

7. **Inappropriate resources**

8. **Unrealistic expectations**

9. **Inadequate knowledge transfer to your people**

10. **Poor project management**

Finally, a methodology contains the collective wisdom of those who produced it, and may even contain this wisdom in the form of helpful *tips*. For example, checklists like the one shown in Exhibit 10.1. These are usually created by consultant teams who have far more collective experience in a number of different company and organizational settings than any one company has in its information technology organization.

Exhibit 10.2 shows these "Five T" benefits.

A Few Words of Warning

There are three important warnings to remember when using a methodology.

1. A methodology is a generic approach. It will not prescriptively solve all of a company's problems because, while it is generally true, it is never specifically accurate. Each company has some

Exhibit 10.2   Five Ts

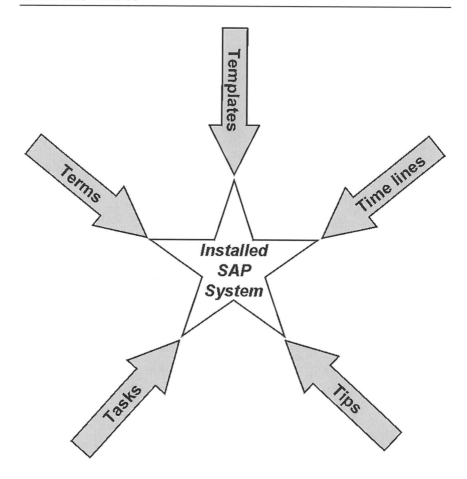

unique aspects, and every R/3 implementation will be affected by the particulars of the organization.

2. Because every organization is different in both its makeup and its reasons for implementing R/3, a methodology cannot be relied on to such a degree that flexibility is lost.

3. On the one hand, a methodology will not describe every necessary task; on the other hand, following every detail of the methodology may result in unnecessary work.

In short, the methodology must be put into a context of your own business and its needs. Use it with an understanding of your needs by adopting those aspects that support your goals and discarding those that do not.

SIMILARITIES IN ALL R/3 METHODOLOGIES

All methodologies for implementing SAP software have a few common elements.

First, and most important, they are all structured. They consist of phases, which are broken down into tasks, further broken down into activities and finally into worksteps.

Almost all methodologies have four phases, which may have different names, but can generally be thought of as follows:

1. *Initiate.* This phase includes planning and costing the effort, determining the internal staff and outside help necessary, defining the scope of the implementation, and doing the initial business-case justification for the undertaking.
2. *Think.* This is the phase in which the current or "as-is" state of both systems and processes is analyzed and what is wanted from the "to-be" state determined.
3. *Work.* In this phase, the R/3 program is actually configured to the specifics of a company's business, then tested and deployed.
4. *Watch.* The watch phase entails measuring the results achieved against the expectations, and supporting, maintaining, and upgrading the system as necessary.

Exhibit 10.3 illustrates these phases.

SAP'S ASAP METHODOLOGY

SAP has developed its own methodology, Accelerated SAP (ASAP), which differs from most other methodologies in a few ways.

Exhibit 10.3   The Four Common Methodology Phases

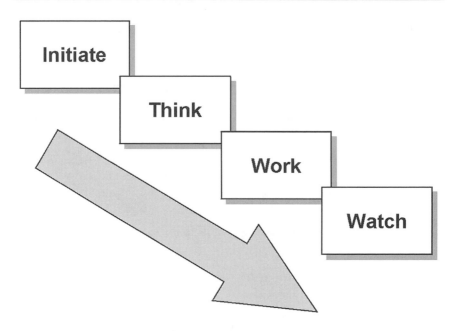

First, it is designed for simple SAP installations by companies that are less complex and smaller in size than the enormous, global companies that have turned to SAP in the past. It works best for a business or business unit that generates between $200 million and $2 billion in revenue as a single-country or regional entity.

Second, the ASAP methodology is designed to be followed rigorously. Other differences include the following:

- o There is no analysis done of the "as is"; you go directly to designing the "to-be" system.
- o There is no coincident process re-engineering or redesign—you accept the SAP process definitions as is. In this way, R/3 completely drives the way your business processes work in the future.
- o It works only for the core modules of R/3, such as finance, sales and distribution, and control. For example, it does not integrate

legacy logistics, incorporate electronic data interchange (EDI), or integrate project systems.

o You must be business ready, meaning the business has to be able to jump right in without any complex change management exercises.

o You move directly to production. There is no prototyping or proof of concept.

o There is no linkage to business or information systems strategy. The assumption is that the decision to go with SAP software is final and correct.

For companies that can live with these constraints, SAP believes its methodology can bring them to the point of a full implementation within six to nine months, less than half the time it often takes to do a more complex implementation.

The six phases of ASAP are simple:

1. *Project Preparation* launches the project team.
2. The *Business Blueprint* is an outline of what the to-be business and SAP system state will look like.
3. *Simulation* is designing and configuring the R/3 system.
4. *Validation* is testing.
5. In *Final Preparation* and *Go-Live,* the necessary interfaces and conversions are written and the system turned on.
6. *Support* is the ongoing maintenance, operations, and upgrading of the R/3 system.

SUMMIT R/3 METHODOLOGY

Summit R/3 is a composite method that is built on top of and encompasses other Coopers & Lybrand (C&L) methodologies, while containing specific SAP guidance. Exhibit 10.4 shows how Summit R/3 fits into the full family of C&L methodologies.

From the beginning, Summit R/3 was designed to include the best of other methodologies. Our idea was simple: We do not need to repeat the

Exhibit 10.4   Summit R/3 Building Blocks

Summit R/3 is a composite method which is built on top of and encompasses other C&L methods while also containing specific SAP guidance.

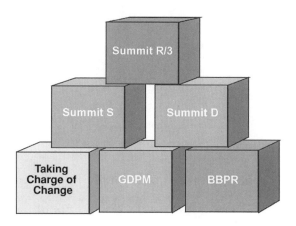

excellent work of colleagues working in complementary areas. We have now extended this concept to SAP's ASAP methodology, incorporating key areas of ASAP into our Summit R/3 methodology.

Exhibit 10.5 shows the Summit R/3 methodology at its top level of detail. What differentiates C&L's methodologies from many others is not so much the names of the discrete phases (left of diagram) but the continuous activities that cut across those phases.

Our approach to assisting with SAP R/3 implementations is designed to ensure the earliest possible delivery of business benefits. This is accomplished by an up-front focus on defining the target benefits and key performance indicators, as well as building a strong business case for the implementation. (The need for a strong business case and how to develop one is described in some detail in Chapter 2.)

We also focus on strong cultural change management and project management. Implementation success is tracked against the strategic analysis and rigorous process design that is done up front in the effort. A regular user review of process design and prototyping outputs is conducted, breaking the work into standard pieces in order to provide both team focus and a reliable scale for measuring progress.

We also use the "80/20" approach to scoping, planning, business process, and design decisions, using prior experience and inherent exper-

Exhibit 10.5   Summit R/3 Overview

Discrete Phases	**Continuous Activities**					
Initiation						
Strategy Analysis	Integration Management	Knowledge Transfer	Technical Architecture	Performance Measurements	Project Management	Change Management
Process Design						
Prototype						
Develop						
Transition						
Sustain						

tise to gauge which 20 percent of the possible implementation activities will result in 80 percent of the desired results.

Scope, budget, and time scales are defined early in the effort. There is not infinite flexibility. Our philosophy and approach allows a company to plan effectively, creating the best possible achievable project plans that accurately reflect requirements in each of these three areas. It also allows a company to manage and execute plans effectively, so progress can be monitored and corrected, if necessary.

Knowledge Transfer

Knowledge transfer is the key to our approach. SAP is not something that a company can have done for it, or to it. Rather, the company must do it by using the consultants it hires as coaches and as a source of knowledge and experience.

Consulting teams are staffed with a mix of industry, IT, BPR, project management, and specialist skills so that a company may draw on all of those resources, transferring knowledge from the consulting force to the company's own project team.

Exhibit 10.6   Using Summit R/3 to Create a New Business Architecture

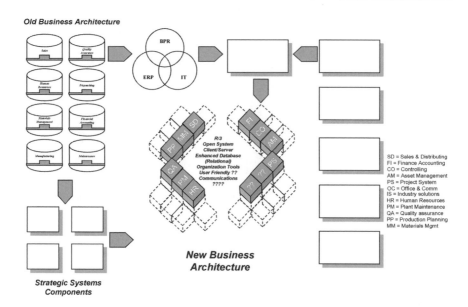

Exhibit 10.6 shows how our proprietary methodology, Summit R/3, integrates IT strategy, BPR, and implementation of SAP software to create a new business architecture.

The enterprise-wide design phase incorporates all of the preparation, design, and prototyping work necessary to develop an agreed-upon set of documented global "to-be" processes and a fully configured system that can be demonstrated as fully supportive of these processes.

The staged implementation is carried out by first implementing one module, as agreed to in the implementation strategy, developing the prototype system into a production system, going live with this system, and sustaining live operations. This procedure is then repeated until all planning implementations are completed.

It cannot be stressed enough how important it is that the enterprise-wide design phase truly represent an enterprise solution, so that process designs and table configurations do not need to be changed for each subsequent aspect of the implementation as one module cascades into another.

The specifics of the implementation timetable will be discussed in Chapters 15 and 16.

Six Keys of Success

Our approach has six additional pieces that are present across the entire project life cycle. They are the keys to successful implementation. These are the continuous activities shown in Exhibit 10.5.

1. *Integration Management* validates project phasing and covers the actions that have to be taken throughout the project to ensure that the SAP R/3 modules are integrated with one another, with bolt-on software, and with legacy systems that remain.
2. *Knowledge Transfer* ensures that at each stage the project team, user community, and support teams all have appropriate skills and knowledge about the SAP R/3 business functionality and technical capabilities.
3. *Technical Architecture* ensures that the hardware and software necessary to support an SAP implementation is available when it is required by the project. This includes planning, sizing, and purchasing and installing processors, storage, communications, desktop personal computers (PCs), and software appropriate to the development, test and production environments. In addition, Technical Architecture should include operational procedures that maintain the integrity of each of these environments.
4. *Performance Measurement* is established to measure the project's progression through a series of intermediate milestones established in the design phase. By measuring progress closely, mistakes and false starts can be acknowledged early, necessary changes can be made, and the costs of implementation process problems can be kept to a minimum.
5. *Project Management* is performed in conjunction with the company's program and project management (discussed in Chapter 12.) Our project management approach provides a mechanism for integrating the activities of project team members, as well as for resolving conflicts and disputes between members and various teams within the project who may be seeking to optimize their own work while running the risk of suboptimizing the entire effort.

117

6. *Change Management* seeks to ensure that the corporate culture is able to accept the changes in work life that will accompany the technical changes brought on by use of SAP's R/3 software, and by the increased business integration. (Change management is discussed in detail in Chapter 13.)

11

Tools

The term *tool* is used in many ways in discussions of SAP software. However, we use the word tool to mean something specific in an SAP environment. We define a tool as any software other than SAP's R/3 that is used to enhance R/3's implementation or basic functionality, such as reporting.

A tool is not the same as a bolt-on, which is a piece of software that can be used in conjunction with R/3 in order to perform a task that R/3 itself is not capable of.

An example of an interfacing tool is Mercator, while Vertex is an example of a bolt-on package used for providing U.S. sales and use tax functionality.

There are literally hundreds of tools and pieces of bolt-on software available, with more becoming available every month.

There are basically two different types of tools—those used by the implementation team and those used by end users.

IMPLEMENTATION TEAM TOOLS

The implementation project team has five different types of tools it can use in the R/3 implementation effort.

Methodology tools
Documentation tools

Programming and interface tools

Configuration tools

Training tools

All of these implementation tools can reduce the time it takes to implement the software and consequently the cost of a successful implementation. While SAP has developed some tools, most tools have been developed by third parties. There may be several tools that do the same thing, their differences being the degree of elegance in the technique used to perform the task and the price. Many consulting firms that are partners with SAP bring to an R/3 installation assignment a group of proprietary tools. This is especially true of methodology tools.

When it receives a prototype of a new tool, SAP performs some quality assurance on the tool, and if the company believes the tool can be helpful, it then sanctions its use and includes the third-party provider in its list of so-called Logo Partners. SAP does not, however, do any quality assurance work on methodology tools, although it stresses the use of its own methodology, Accelerated SAP (ASAP), in conjunction with others to ensure some level of consistency.

Methodology Tools

Exhibit 11.1 shows how the ASAP methodology meshes with Coopers & Lybrand's (C&L's) own Summit R/3 methodology. Methodologies are provided in a variety of formats, from simple manuals and books to sophisticated software with links to other packages (e.g., MS Project).

When we talk about methodology tools, we are talking about tools that help use the methodology, such as software and guides. Methodology tools are primarily proprietary tools brought to an assignment by an implementation consultant. They are large tools that guide the project implementation team through the implementation process, providing a game plan for accomplishing the tasks involved in the implementation. The emphasis of most methodologies is on implementing the system from design to cut over.

Many times a consulting firm's implementation methodology locks neatly together with other methodologies for information systems (IS)

Exhibit 11.1 SUMMIT R/3 and ASAP

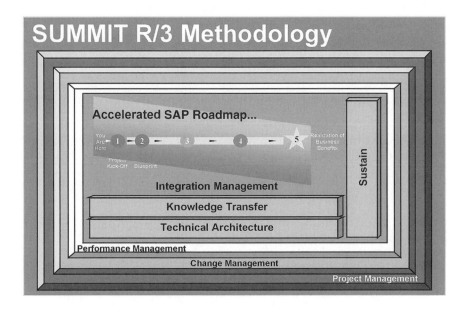

strategy, system maintenance, change management and so on. For instance, at Coopers & Lybrand, our methodologies are given the name Summit. We have, among other pieces of the Summit methodology library, Summit S for IS strategy, Summit D for system design, Summit R/3 for SAP R/3 implementation, and Summit M for system maintenance.

Some companies will sell a methodology tool off the shelf with no consulting services while others will provide only the methodology as an adjunct to a consulting assignment. Some methodology tools are proprietary while others are commercial, and the customer can modify them.

Documentation Tools

These tools provide templates for designing documentation, including system change approval documentation and system change management documents.

Again, these tools can be proprietary or commercial and may even be developed in-house. We have helped a number of clients develop Lotus Notes–based documentation databases. These act as a project repository, a standard software tool, and a means of communication. They range in price from a few hundred dollars to many thousands of dollars. They range in complexity from simple templates that allow one to create documents of the system configurations to complex process modelers that use SAP standard nomenclature and configure the appropriate tables from the information fed into the tool.

Exhibit 11.2 shows the most common type of SAP standard diagram, a process flow of the event-driven process chain (EPC) diagram.

This diagram links a series of business events with the processes they go through. At the lower level of detail, a process box is mapped to an individual transaction, and the events produced by these are represented by SAP reports or documents.

Programming and Interface Tools

Between one third and one half of the cost of an SAP R/3 implementation is taken up by writing conversion and interface routines from legacy systems to SAP. These conversion and interface routines are labor-intensive programming jobs that entail writing almost endless code.

Increasingly, tools are being developed that perform the code generation automatically. These sophisticated tools allow you to point and click, telling the software the legacy system you are moving away from the data fields that you will want to use in the SAP software, and the software writes the code.

An example of this kind of tool is IBM's Data Migrator.

Configuration Tools

SAP is investing heavily in the development of configuration tools that assist in the time-consuming and expensive task of configuring the system. These vary from the more simple functionality guides to process-flow automated configuration. Again, the Livemodel package is a prime example of this type of software.

SAP has developed the Implementation Guide (IMG), a table-by-table walkthrough of the system configuration. This is taken further with the development of the Business Engineer in R/4, which uses a question-

Exhibit 11.2 An Example of an EPC Diagram

Exhibit 11.3   Business Navigator

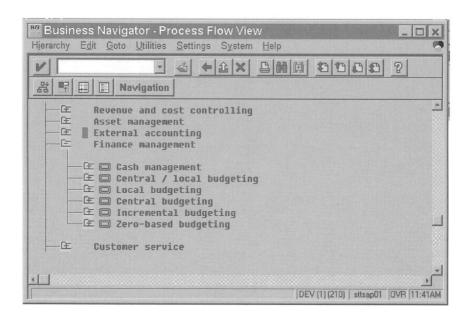

and-answer approach to guide the user through configuration and includes process models in the Business Navigator. A screen from the Business Navigator is shown in Exhibit 11.3.

Ultimately, the goal is to configure the system directly and automatically from process diagrams. Livemodel leads the field in this area.

Training Tools

Experience shows that it takes 40 hours to write one hour of customized end-user training. The use of training tools can reduce this to four to six hours of development time for each hour of training.

Training is usually done by computer-based simulation, often using CD-ROM. Companies are developing "canned" training programs that present typical R/3 screens, which can then be customized to look like the kind of transaction information the particular company will be looking at.

The market is increasing rapidly as more companies find that the development of training materials is time consuming and costly. As the market increases, this is pushing more companies to develop training tools.

END-USER TOOLS

End-user tools provide functions to business users and the information technology (IT) professionals supporting the SAP system and the surrounding architecture.

End-user tools fall into the following four categories:

1. Reporting and warehousing
2. Archiving
3. System and network management
4. Communications

Reporting and warehousing tools serve to add functionality and usability to the system by allowing end users to build customized reports across R/3 modules and databases, and even across systems, including R/2, R/3, and legacy systems. Instead of having to develop a data warehouse, some of these tools can be used to download into spreadsheet formats, which finance people especially are used to working with.

These tools are gaining a wide following with more sophisticated finance users, especially internal auditors. The point-and-click method is easier than using SAP's own report writer and the advanced business application programming (ABAP) language.

Archiving tools provide the IS function with backup and recovery facilities across a variety of software and hardware platforms.

System and network management tools monitor the overall enterprise systems architecture and simplify communications between systems. These will be discussed in greater detail in Chapter 19.

Communications tools allow SAP to "talk" to other applications and users, using a variety of methods including electronic data interchange (EDI), voice, telephone, and Internet. A wide variety of such tools exist and are used for many different applications.

BOLT-ON SOFTWARE

Bolt-on software is software that can be used in conjunction with SAP's R/3 to perform tasks and functions outside of the software's ability. Bolt-ons are licensed by SAP. Most bolt-ons are developed by software companies with long histories, and in many instances they are adaptations of the company's software to run in conjunction with R/3.

Examples of areas in which bolt-on software is common are in U.S. sales and use tax, imaging packages, and in computer-aided design (CAD) systems.

12

Process Redesign

As discussed in earlier chapters, one of the ways SAP separates its software from other enterprise solution software is that R/3 almost forces a company to redesign its business processes. In this chapter, a little about how and why that is will be discussed.

In order to understand more about why redesign can be accomplished post-software decision, while re-engineering cannot, it is important to have firm definitions of process redesign and process re-engineering.

Process redesign is *changing strategic value-added business processes and the systems, policies, and organizational structures that support them, in order to optimize productivity and the flow of work.* See Exhibit 12.1.

Process re-engineering is the *fundamental analysis and radical redesigning of business practices and management systems, job definitions, organizational systems, and beliefs and behaviors in order to achieve dramatic performance improvement.*

The goal of process redesign is to eliminate non–value-adding work, not necessarily to eliminate jobs. Process redesign that is enabled by Enterprise Resource Planning (ERP) software also allows automation of much low–value-adding work.

Elimination of non–value-adding work and minimization and automation of low–value-adding work, in turn, turns loose employee energy to be spent on truly value-adding work and can dramatically increase productive capacity.

Exhibit 12.1   The Components of Process Redesign

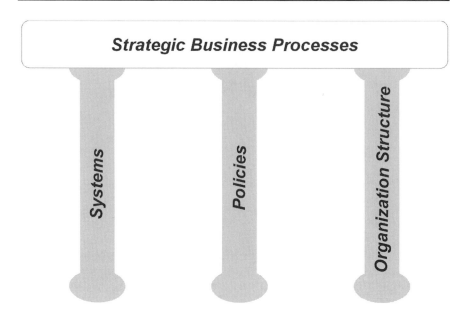

Too often, process redesign or re-engineering has been used as a cover by executives to initiate a downsizing. In the best circumstances, the efficiencies gained through process redesign are used to free up individuals to perform more value-adding work in order to increase the company's bottom line.

What a business process redesign entails differs from one company to the next, but there are a few common themes (see Exhibit 12.2).

- o Process redesign means forgetting about old business practices.
- o Process redesign is organized around continuous business processes aimed at getting products to customers. Remember, customer facing processes tie to the businesses strategy.
- o Far more often than not as we enter the twenty-first century, business process redesign is about applying increasingly sophisticated information technology (IT). Specifically, for our discussion, process redesign refers to applying SAP software.

Exhibit 12.2   Process Redesign Themes

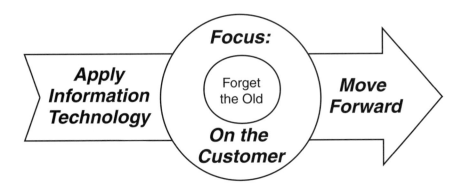

The key driver of process redesign is the need to improve the company's financial performance by improving operational performance. It is a realization that the numbers don't magically appear and that long-term financial gains can occur only when a company delivers increasing customer value while simultaneously lowering the cost of delivering that value.

Process redesign aims at four things simultaneously: a reduction in process costs and time, and a simultaneous improvement in quality and customer service. This is called the "value equation."

$$\text{Value} = (\text{quality} \times \text{service})/(\text{cost} \times \text{time})$$

At the same time, process redesign done properly recognizes that striving for more effective and efficient processes increases pressure on workers. Therefore, it includes a lot of education and training for all workers, as well as striving to make the organization one in which workers are increasingly "empowered" to make operational decisions through providing them with a knowledge and understanding of the business and the particular process they are intimately involved with.

Businesses that have not solidified the reasons for and goals of redesign, and the ways to achieve those goals, find that any goals are short lived. Process redesign must be driven from the top down, but it cannot be firmly established only by those at the top.

HOW R/3 HELPS WITH PROCESS REDESIGN

SAP has not set out to enable process redesign for every business process. It has chosen to create enabling software for what it considers to be the most important processes.

Until recently, even companies that were successful in radical reengineering of processes had a difficult time creating effective IT to work with those processes in a timely manner. Before ERP packages, systems had to be custom designed. These customized systems were limited in their scope and size (see Exhibit 12.3).

In short, the pace of business change always outran the pace of enabling software development. Even SAP's R/2 software, the first real ERP software, which was available in the late 1980s, had a difficult time keeping up.

However, that is exactly what R/3 does. SAP's sole goal in its software is to provide automation for the tedious low–value-adding reporting and documenting of business activities. What makes the software stand out above the competition is the degree of integration with which this documentation is done, combined with its breadth of functionality. An entry at the operating level automatically courses its way through the IT veins of the company and posts the resultant data into all of the appropriate places: general ledger postings, reduction in inventory, generation of new order for material, generation of payment for approved invoices, and so on.

In this way, for the first time, a company really can redesign and automate on a large scale at the same time, without having to shut the business down in order to do it.

SAP's R/3 software actually enhances a company's ability to conduct process redesign by virtue of the fact that SAP has defined standard processes and what they entail. There is a language in which process terms mean the same thing to everyone using SAP's software. Armed with the knowledge of what the software tool can do to eliminate the non–value-adding functions (e.g., rekeying data), and automate much of the low–value-adding reporting (e.g., three-way matches), one can then examine how the value-added aspects of the process can be enhanced.

SAP's integration forces one to focus on redesigning continuous, end-to-end core business processes. The "knock-on" effect of data touching so

Exhibit 12.3   ERP Software Automates Low–Value-Added Processes
              in a Company

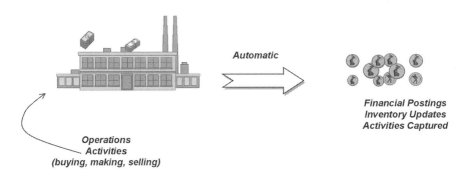

many different nodes within the business means that a piece of a process in isolation literally cannot be redesigned. The entire process must be re-designed.

This, however, is a double-edged sword. Not only does a piece of data flow all the way through a particular process, but it also moves through many processes. Because of this, it is difficult to manage the scope of a redesign effort. One must decide at the front end of the effort just which processes will be redesigned, and admit that other processes will be "left hanging," with SAP touching them but not becoming fully integrated as part of the current effort.

R/3 comes with a set of tools that assist with process redesign. These are on the Business Engineering Workbench. They provide a company with the ability to model and diagram its business processes. This process modeling ability allows performance of a "what if" analysis of possible ways to redesign the process. Manipulating the software to do these what ifs is relatively straightforward. The difficulty comes in making it all work after the decisions have been made.

Assumption Creep and Scope Creep

Scope creep occurs when the scope of the SAP implementation keeps ex-panding during the implementation process itself, as implementation teams find that the software touches business processes that they had not considered when determining the effort's scope.

A similar problem is *assumption creep*. This occurs when various process redesign teams assume that everyone on every other team knows what they know, and defines what will occur at the integration points based on this.

For example, the purchasing team and the finance team may each assume that the other is defining material posting rules. Processes can be defined, configured, and tested independently and appear to be successful. Only when the processes are viewed together in an integrated way is it clear that assumption creep has occurred.

The way to mitigate scope creep is through strong project and program management. Project and program managers must constantly remind implementation teams of the boundaries within which they are working. It involves reining in teams and forcing them to "stick to their knitting" and not cross boundaries where it has been decided that no work will be done while simultaneously managing the integration points.

Assumption creep must be dealt with in a different way. Teams must be forced to communicate, candidly and continuously, about the way they are redesigning their particular process and the assumptions they are making about how their process will interact with all the other processes that other teams are working on.

APPROACHES TO REDESIGN

There are three different ways to thinking about tackling the redesign effort. However, there is a best approach when SAP has been selected as the technological enabler.

First you could redesign your processes and then tackle the R/3 implementation. We don't recommended going about things this way. You lose the ability to take advantage of R/3's special qualities. It will entail additional R/3 implementation costs, since you will be force fitting R/3 into processes already designed to your liking.

Second, you could implement R/3 and then hope for process improvement. However, we cannot give an example in which this has been successful. Again, it will probably result in increased costs as you go through expensive redesign activities while being constricted in your redesign choices by the R/3 software itself.

This is an investment in IT, not an investment in your business. It might happen if the force driving you to consider SAP is the Chief Information Officer (CIO) organization, which seeks to develop SAP skills because it is hot on the market.

Finally, we recommend that you undertake business process redesign in the context of R/3. (Consider R/3 as the enabling medium and take your redesign cues from the medium.)

We use the analogy of a sculptor. A sculptor takes to his project a different vision of what the final sculpture will look like depending on whether the medium is clay, marble, wood, or metal. Each material both limits the final outcome and enhances the artist's opportunities to make the final outcome truly successful.

The same is true with enabling IT. SAP both limits the ultimate outcome of a process redesign and enhances the outcome.

Benefits of what might be thought of as true IT-enabled redesign are many, including the following:

- Lower design costs. You do it right the first time, because the information technology steers you in the right direction.
- More effective use of R/3. Because you understand the constraints and possibilities, you can get every last ounce of value out of the software.
- You are able to align the generic functions of the system with the particular functions of the business.

HOW TO REDESIGN WITH SAP

The key to redesigning within the context of SAP is to start by envisioning the end state, in terms of how discrete processes will look and in terms of how the discrete processes will be integrated through the software's abilities.

You need to confirm that R/3 is indeed the best information technology enabler for you. If you have any doubt of this, you need to go back to rethink your IT strategy.

After confirming R/3 as the enabler, you need to firmly determine the scope of process change you will undertake. The following: the four dimensions you need to determine within the scope:

1. The processes that will be redesigned.
2. Whether those processes will be changed within the entire company or only a portion (i.e., division) of the company.
3. The geographical reach of the redesign (e.g., global, regional, or single-country).
4. Determine which existing information systems will be replaced and which will be retained. This is called the IT topology.

The third major issue in setting up IT-enabled redesign is to create appropriate metrics to measure whether the redesign is achieving the expectations set out for it. These metrics should be stated in terms of either cost, time, quality, or service, or a combination of more than one of those metrics.

Then, it is time to truly establish use of the SAP enterprise model (discussed in detail in Chapter 16). This entails understanding what certain SAP terms mean, such as "plant" and "company code." Picturing the end state of the redesign with a firm understanding of SAP terminology fully sets the context for the effort.

In an SAP-enabled redesign, we put much less stress than many earlier adherents of redesign on understanding, mapping, and documenting the company's "as-is" state. You need to achieve only a high-level understanding of current systems, organization structure, and process flows. It is necessary, however, to put a little more detailed effort into understanding your business's product hierarchy and associated product costs (i.e., cost of materials, labor, and administration).

DESIGNING THE TO-BE STATE

The "to-be" or desired state must be designed along three dimensions: (1) processes, (2) organization, and (3) systems.

Early adherents to process re-engineering argued generally that the processes must be designed and the systems carried along as adjuncts, added on to assist the process reorganization.

When we talk about SAP and redesign, because of its tight integration and the fact that it is an enterprise solution, we urge you to design the systems when you design the process.

Processes

Once you have a relatively good understanding of both SAP's standard process language and of your "as-is" processes, you need to compare and contrast the standard processes denoted in R/3 with the way your processes operate today. You can look for ways that R/3 can naturally improve the current state.

R/3 eliminates redundancies. Today, especially in large corporations, there may be multiple systems that do the same thing (e.g., accounts receivable) across business units. With R/3, a single system can do accounts receivable across the entire enterprise.

R/3 can automate and eliminate human labor, or it can augment human labor, allowing that labor to become more effective. For instance, by automatically posting to the general ledger, moving data from one place to another without human intervention, people's time is freed up to aggregate the data into meaningful information and to do more complex analysis of that information in order to make better business decisions.

R/3 can change the sequence of functions. No longer is an end-of-month or end-of-year book close dependent on a particular sequence of "roll-up" tasks that takes 10 or 12 business days. SAP software can collapse time lines and do it in a single day, or can even allow the company to perform a "soft close," essentially closing in real time.

In a similar way, R/3 eliminates a lot of intermediate paperwork steps in work flow. Data and information can be automatically routed to the appropriate person for review and approval. No longer will it need to go to an individual whose sole function is to route things to the proper decision maker; the system can be configured to route automatically.

Also, R/3 allows you to operate efficiently over a wider geographical area by consolidating coding (e.g., vendors, material number, and customer number). No longer will one customer have 12 customer numbers because you deal with 12 different business units, or one supplier have 12 vendor numbers because 12 of your business units purchase supplies from the same supplier.

All ERP software, not just R/3, gives one the ability to capitalize on instantaneous communications, the ability to perform work in parallel, and the ability to share information across formerly discrete functions. R/3 is the most fully integrative of all the ERP software available today.

Organization

Too often, those who run either a process redesign effort or a systems enhancement effort leap right to working on the processes or the systems without giving enough consideration to the effects that the effort's outcome will have on the people who ultimately will have to do the work within the process or who work with the system.

Coincident with the design of the process at an activity level, a new human resource structure must be designed, role by role. As well, one should have an understanding of what the costs will be to train individuals and to manage the change in terms of reduced productivity during the period of change—counseling, retraining those who will stay, separating those who will not, and hiring those who bring new and necessary skill sets to the redesigned processes.

Systems

You must have a firm grasp of which of your current systems—both hardware and software—will be supplanted by R/3 and, as importantly, which will not.

This leads you to determining which data and information will need to be passed back and forth between R/3 to the legacy systems that will remain. In order to make those handoffs successful, you need to understand the conversions and interfaces that will need to be developed.

You need to develop a firm deployment plan. Deployment can be done in a number of ways—rolling out the system function by function across the organization; fully functional one business unit at a time, one region at a time, or one country at a time; or one function at a time one business unit at a time, one region at a time, or one country at a time.

Along with the deployment plan, you need to come up with some fairly well-determined estimates of what the systems-change effort will cost in both cash and personpower. This is necessary as both a way to cement realistic expectations on the part of executive management of what the effort will entail, and as a benchmark against which interim measurements can be made.

DOCUMENTING THE TO-BE STATE

It is important that all of your work in redesigning systems, structures, and processes be fully documented. In order to do this, you need to map both the SAP functionality that you utilize as well as the processes you redesign.

Documentation includes that necessary for end users of the process and the system, for those who will maintain and upgrade the system and process over time, and for those who must manage both end users and maintainers.

In other words, there is technical documentation, end-user documentation, and human resource documentation necessary. Human resource documentation includes new performance measures and key success factors for individuals' work.

FOUR KEYS TO SUCCESS

There are four keys to success in IT-enabled process redesigning.

1. **Look for the big wins.** If you're going to spend all the time, money, and human effort necessary to implement SAP's R/3, you need to show some success. Look for improvement in things you do poorly and SAP does naturally well.

2. **Keep the value equation in mind.** The big win needs to be seen in one of the four variables of the value equation: Value = (quality × service)/(cost × time).

3. **Measure the expected improvements.** In the end, you must be able to quantify how operations, and the concomitant financial measures, have improved.

4. **Keep SAP R/3 capabilities in mind.** Exploit the software! The software can be truly exploited only when it is implemented properly to begin with.

13

Risk Management

Every action taken in business entails some level of risk. While it is impossible to eliminate all risk from any business undertaking, least of all from one so radical as process change and large-scale business software implementation, it is possible to manage risk in a way that allows a business to pursue its legitimate opportunities without endangering its survival.

SAP projects, by their very nature, are fraught with risk. An SAP project is not just a software implementation project; rather, it is a major change initiative. With proper focus, the risks of an SAP implementation can be mitigated. However, to do this, the risks must be identified and managed.

Risk management is as old as the recorded history of warfare. The Roman Army had rules for building its nightly encampments. A key rule was that half the men built the defensive position while the other half acted as watchmen, guarding against the risk of attack.

Our definition of risk is *any factor that can affect the ability of the project to deliver results that are on time and on budget, and that meet expectations.*

FOUR STEPS IN THE RISK MANAGEMENT PROCESS

Risk is essentially uncertainty. Uncertainty can be described in a mathematical way. For instance, if I toss a coin, I am 50 percent certain it will come up heads. As the number of variables in the equation increases, the level of uncertainty grows. Therefore, the number of possible risks grows. Risk management becomes more complex, and more important.

Risks come in one of the following six different varieties:

1. Executive risks
2. Project management and project plan risks
3. Chief information officer (CIO) organization/technical risks
4. Organizational (end users in functional areas) risk
5. Decision making risks
6. Functional risks

Overlaying these different varieties of risk are the following four aspects of risk management, which, taken together, can be viewed as the risk management process:

1. Risk identification
2. Risk assessment and analysis
3. Risk control and mitigation
4. Risk avoidance

Risk management must be a part of process change and software implementation from the beginning of the project. It must also be participative and iterative, meaning that all participants in the undertaking know of the risk management plans, think about them, and add to them as time goes on, making the risk management effort better over time.

Risk management is an easily overlooked part of the project planning process. For instance, one company implementing SAP failed to undertake risk analysis. Subsequently, the project leadership was blind sided when risks materialized and required constant fire fighting. Other implementations face the same problems, but with a risk management plan they are able to nip them in the bud.

Not engaging in risk management from the start can be catastrophic. Conducting risk identification, assessment, and analysis early on provides an opportunity to achieve buy-in from all elements of the company—

Exhibit 13.1 The Risk Management Loop

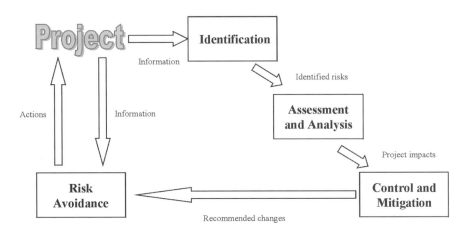

executives, project teams, and end users. This, in turn, avoids the "I told you so's" as the project progresses and runs up against the unavoidable snags.

Exhibit 13.1 shows the risk management process as a feedback loop.

Risk Identification

Risk identification involves looking at risks on six dimensions: (1) executive; (2) the project plan and project management; (3) the CIO and technical areas; (4) organizational (acceptance within the functional areas); (5) decision making; and (6) the business strategy.

When identifying each risk, it is important to specify within which business area the risk lies, and at what organizational level. This assists in both clarifying the risk and developing actions to control and avoid the risk.

Risks inherent in the decision-making process are especially difficult to mitigate against. Process change and large-scale software implementation cry out for a clear, orderly decision-making process—one in which input is accepted by those with the authority and responsibility for the decisions, and the decisions are made in a timely way.

Long decision cycles; excess time arguing about the decision; and, most of all, backing away from decisions cause confusion, anxiety, and anger within the organization. This triggers other problems, which can drive an effort to failure.

Risks are often difficult to spot. Many are so bound up in the organization's culture that an outsider cannot find them and an insider is so used to them that they do not make an impression. Trying to get a comprehensive picture of all possible risks is akin to herding cats. For that reason, constant re-evaluation of near-term and longer-term risks is the key to success.

Risk Assessment and Analysis

Assessing and analyzing risks means determining their potential impact on the project, as well as their likelihood of happening. The impact on the project can be in terms of missed milestones, the need for rework, the need for re-implementation, and the level of acceptance the project will have after it is completed.

Exhibit 13.2 shows the potential impact and likelihood of occurrence for each of the six varieties of risk.

Executive Risks. These are risks regarding executive commitment and support, including sponsorship, alignment with other business initiatives, and turf fighting (e.g., finance vs. operations.)

These risks have a high impact on both the project team and its work, as well as on delivery of the implementation. The likelihood of occurrence is higher if there is less prework by the leadership team and if the software implementation is being carried out for unclear or conflicting reasons.

Project Management and Project Plan Risks. These are risks that affect the efficiency and effectiveness of how the project is run. An SAP R/3 implementation is one of the largest programs a company will ever undertake; it will certainly be the largest systems implementation a company has ever undertaken to date. Such an effort cries out for effective program and project management.

The most apparent risks in this area include planning and execution of project steps, as well as knowledge transfer from experienced staff or outside consultants to those who will carry out the project and later retention of this newly knowledgeable staff. Other risks in this category are the

Exhibit 13.2   Key Risk Categories

Type Of Risk	Impact	Probability
Executive		
Project Management		
Technical		
Organization		
Decision Making		
Functional		

scope of the project (watch out for scope creep), adherence to methodology, and use of resources.

These risks can have a very high impact on both the project team and delivery. The likelihood of occurrence is high.

Chief Information Officer Organization/Technical Risks.   There are real issues of hardware, software, and systems architecture involved in an SAP R/3 implementation. While the exercise must be driven by business needs and not by information technology (IT) desires, it is important that the technical organization remain part of the leadership team for the project. If they drop off, technical risks may never be addressed.

Technical risks include sizing, networks, and PC requirements. For example, one company's IT department was given money to upgrade the communications at remote sites, but used the money on another project. When SAP software was installed, the CIO did not tell those running the installation project that the remote network had not been upgraded. When the software was fully installed, an operator pressed the key to send some information to a remote location and nothing happened for two minutes—the time it took the network to transmit.

More organizational risks in the CIO organization include creating the skills to support SAP software, as well as retaining skills both to support SAP and to create legacy interfaces as needed, and, finally, to turn off legacy systems and move fully to the R/3 environment.

The impact of technical risks varies; it can affect end users from individuals to the entire organization. Chief Information Officer organizational risks have organization-wide affects. The likelihood of all of these risks occurring increases as the CIO organization involvement decreases.

Organizational (End Users in Functional Areas). If the entire organization is not aligned with the project, different functional areas may retain their old ways of doing business. These disconnects hurt the overall integration of the business process and lead to gaps in functionality, a reliance on future releases, and the need for custom development to create a mirror of the way employees operate. There must be adequate training and change management in order to create user acceptance. Staff retention is also an issue: If the most knowledgeable staff leave or have a negative view of the project, it is hard to keep the rest on track.

These risks have a high impact on specific areas but also affect other areas. The likelihood of occurrence varies depending on how much attention is paid to understanding the organizational culture and creating viable ways to decrease resistance.

Decision-making Risks. A poor decision-making process, slow decision making, or the inability to make crucial decisions can hamper the R/3 installation effort. It is crucial to keep momentum going throughout the effort, and the only way to do that is to make decisions that move the project toward the next milestone.

These risks have a high impact on the entire organization. Their likelihood of occurring is low, but the impact for those occurrences that do happen is very high.

Functional Risks. Functional risks are those that affect the system's ability to support specific users or user functions. Typically, functional risks occur where specific requirements or business processes are overlooked in the system implementation, where promised functionality does not appear in new releases, or where custom developments do not meet user requirements. It is common for such risks to occur in limited areas of an SAP project, especially where the scope of the project is wide or poorly defined. Their impact is high, within limited areas.

Risk Control and Mitigation

Risk can be controlled through a number of different strategies and actions. It is important to think through a clear, coherent strategy for risk control before undertaking any of the specific actions.

Since an SAP R/3 project entails a host of risks, ranging from the purely technical to what happens when the most basic of human emotions are triggered, a comprehensive risk-control strategy is important. Within this strategy can be detailed a number of actions to be taken to alleviate the risk in each of the six major risk categories.

Risk control must be constantly monitored. A good way to start is to step back when each project milestone is reached and assess the effectiveness of risk-control actions taken during the time it took to reach the milestone. Revisit identifying and assessing the risks that may dominate the next milestone phase, and determine if the current risk-control strategy and actions will serve well during the next phase, or if a new strategy should be developed and new actions outlined.

Risk Avoidance

It is possible to avoid some risks. This is mostly done by being brutally realistic about the nature and amount of resources it will take to successfully complete a project. It is important that executives and key users define their expectations for the project up front, and for the functionality of the system when it is installed. Then, the project leader must be completely

Exhibit 13.3   Top 10 Risks to an SAP R/3 Project

1.   Inadequate sponsorship

2.   Poor/slow decision making

3.   Poor/no scope definition

4.   Inadequate attention to change management

5.   Lack of cooperation between business areas/departments

6.   Poor use of consultants

7.   Inappropriate resources

8.   Unrealistic expectations

9.   Inadequate knowledge transfer to your people

10.   Poor project management

honest in telling those executives and key users what kind of costs and time commitment are necessary to undertake the project. In our experience, many SAP projects face risks similar to those listed in Exhibit 13.3.

There are costs in people's time, dollars, and technology. These costs must be borne in order to avoid unnecessary risks. Trying to cut corners increases the likelihood of risks occurring and magnifies the impact, and the cost, when they do occur.

14

Project and Program Management

What is the difference between project and program management? Project management is *the day-to-day responsibility for the planning, control, and execution of an individual project.* Program management is *coordination and integration of the goals, objectives, and results of individual projects to achieve the overall business objectives.*

PROJECT MANAGEMENT

The qualities of good program and project managers were discussed in Chapter 4, so in this chapter the focus will be more on the form and function of the project management role. The project manager must perform a number of diverse tasks throughout the project life cycle, as shown in Exhibit 14.1.

Good project managers possess a number of attributes and qualities.

o They are intelligent.
o They communicate well.
o They are respected throughout the organization.
o They are experienced.
o They are good cheerleaders.

Exhibit 14.1   The Project Manager's Tasks

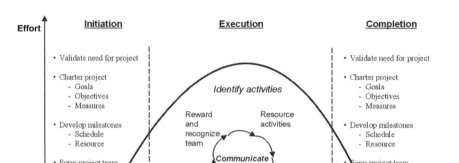

o They are "helicopter thinkers," able to take a broad view from high above the playing field, then zoom down from one subject to another, getting into the detail of various parts of the action when necessary.

Remember, they are the external face of the project. They must present the project to the rank and file within the department, function, or business unit within which they work, as well as to the rest of the company. A good project manager is able to evaluate the conflicts, seek a win–win solution and, if necessary, make a decision that all parties can live with, even those who "lose."

Because SAP software is complex, and the implementation of an SAP system solution is a complex undertaking, project managers for R/3 projects need to have the following five qualities above and beyond the generic project management qualities:

1. **They must be flexible.**   Managing an SAP installation is akin to herding cats. At times, the software seems to have a mind of its own. In addition, every time it touches another piece of the business process, that newest touch point becomes "it," as if the project were an endless game of tag.

2. **They must be determined.**   There will be many hurdles in the project, some natural as part of a complex undertaking, but many of the organizational culture and resistance to change variety. Project managers must have the finesse of a football halfback, weaving and dodging, as well as the toughness of a fullback, able to get "three yards and a cloud of dust" when necessary.

3. **They must be enthusiastic.**   An SAP installation is a long process, and the enthusiasm of many team members will wax and wane over time. Project managers cannot allow the down days to set the tone. They must leave the frustration in the office at the end of the day, and come back the next day ready to do battle again.

4. **They must be personable.**   Team members come in all shapes and sizes, and project managers get along with them all. They need to be able to charm corporate steering committee members as well as rank-and-file workers within the department, function, or business unit in which they are managing the project.

5. **Finally, they must be political.**   They need to know their organization and how to maneuver politically through it.

If a project manager is uncertain about whether he or she has any of these qualities, it's important to find a good second-in-command who is strong in the project manager's weak points and can pick up the slack.

PROJECT STRUCTURES

Most companies are structured either hierarchically or in a matrix. Consequently, they tend to run their projects that way as well. Exhibit 14.2 shows a typical hierarchical project structure.

The hierarchical project structure is the most common approach. It tends to work well in most business cultures, even those that have more of a matrix management structure. It tends not to work in a culture that is a true "consensus" organization.

Exhibit 14.2   Typical Hierarchical Project Structure

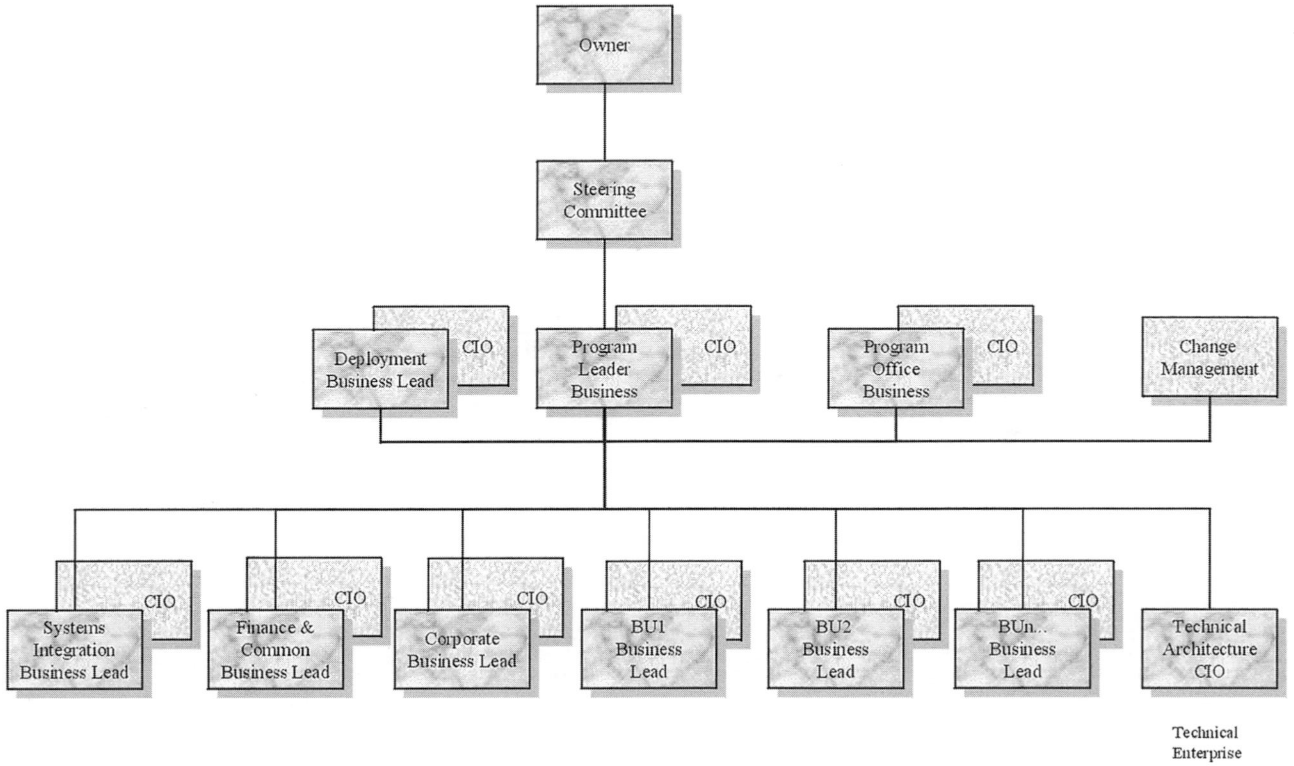

A hierarchical structure is favored for rapid implementation, as it favors chain-of-command decision making. Typically, subteams are created by their particular function. Each team is comprised of the resources it needs to deliver the finished product; for instance, the finance team will have expertise in design, configuration, testing, conversion, documentation, and training. Because of this need for all specialties in each team, hierarchical structure often requires a lot of resources. The structure allows for the role of each person to be defined; there is nowhere to hide.

In a hierarchical structure, the program and project managers have a large integration role.

Exhibit 14.3 shows a matrix project structure.

In a matrix project structure, there are functional teams and there are discipline teams. A true matrix project structure is very free flowing, and allows for the most flexibility and free thinking.

It is possible for individuals to serve on more than one team within a matrix project structure. An individual can serve on a discipline team—say change management—as well as a functional team—finance, for instance. The downside of matrix project management is that people are spread thin and there can be difficulty managing the intersections and crossovers. Also, since people's responsibilities often overlap, there are cracks within which people can hide.

Most SAP projects run with a hybrid project structure, as depicted in Exhibit 14.4.

The steering committee and the program or project manager (or both) still sit above the teams, as in a hierarchical structure. In addition, there are strong functional teams. It is important to maintain a strong functional structure because SAP software has such a clear effect on each function, and those within the function are best able to understand and manage the process changes necessary.

However, as with the matrix organization, there are some process teams that cut across functional lines. Having these process teams in such areas as change management and integration allows for more effective leveraging of specialized, limited resources, since these specialties don't have to reside in each functional team.

Exhibit 14.3   Typical Matrix Project Structure

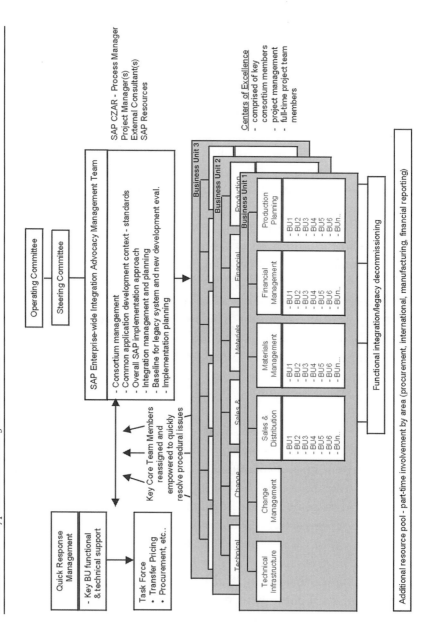

Exhibit 14.4   Common SAP Project Structure

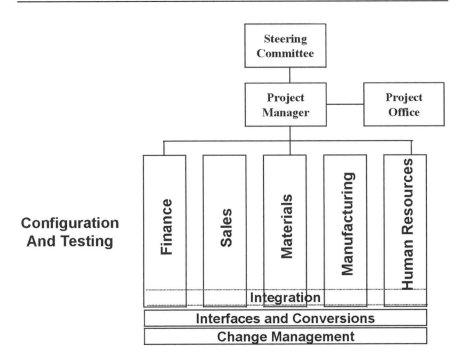

Occasionally, there will be a project that runs in more of a hub-and-spoke type of structure, with an integration team in the center and functional teams around it. This is shown in Exhibit 14.5.

In this scenario, project management resides in the integration hub. One client of ours used this unorthodox structure quite effectively. Weekly integration meetings were used to plan the short- and long-term project goals and activities. These were supplemented by daily issue meetings that were used to identify potential trouble spots for special attention. The project teams were tightly linked and the project was delivered on time and on budget.

Whatever overarching project structure is used, the detailed structure within should reflect the project milestones, tasks, and activities, as seen in Exhibit 14.6.

Exhibit 14.5   Project Management Structure

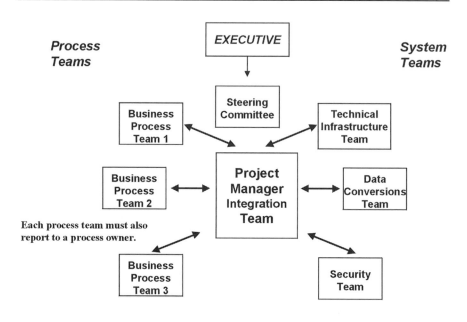

Exhibit 14.6   Detailed Project Plan

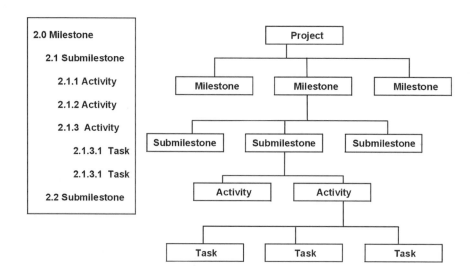

PROJECT PLANNING

Project planning is concerned with three main issues: (1) targets, (2) scope, and (3) resources.

Targets

Implementing R/3 might be seen as akin to trying to eat an elephant. If you try to swallow it in one bite, it will stick in your throat. It is easier to digest if cut into bite-sized pieces.

As discussed in Chapter 6, intermediate targets and milestones should be used throughout a project as part of project management. Determining intermediate targets is, in effect, determining the number and size of the elephant pieces you will eat. Just as the size of a meal is determined by each individual, the targets should be tailored to the individual organization and project. Without setting challenging yet attainable intermediate goals (milestones), it is easy to lose sight of where the end state of the program is. The light at the end of the tunnel seems to be a constantly receding train.

It is also important to understand the individual steps or activities needed to meet a milestone, and the dependencies between targets. Only when this is done can a realistic scenario be created. Exhibit 14.7 shows a sequencing of milestones.

Intermediate goals are important for maintaining a sense of achievement within the teams, and for maintaining realistic expectations on the part of executives who are not involved with the project on a day-to-day basis.

Everyone involved in the project needs intermediate goals, even the project support office. Early goals should be easy, and later goals more difficult, in order to "create wins" soon enough for teams to flex their muscles and develop their team strength.

Scope

Understanding the project's scope from the beginning is critically important. If the scope of the project and program has not been defined, agreed to, and authorized by executive management, disaster awaits.

Exhibit 14.7   Understanding Dependencies

Equally important as each individual milestone is the path taken between milestones to reach the final objective.

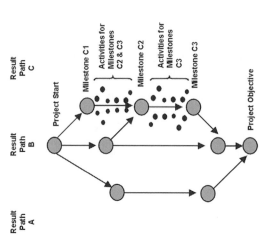

Benefits of a result path:

- Shows the logical connection between milestones;
- Balances technical, cultural, time, cost and quality objectives
- Displays parallel milestones

Because SAP software is so highly integrated, whenever it touches a process, there is the possibility of redesigning that process to utilize the software to a greater extent. If there are boundaries to the scope, however, the project manager can say, "We're not going to do that; it's beyond our scope."

It is important to know up front the number of business processes that will be redesigned and the functions within which SAP software will be implemented. In addition, it is necessary to know the number of legacy systems that will be turned off when the new system is up and running, and where those systems reside. One must know whenever there are geographic, divisional, and functional boundaries for the implementation.

The scope must be clearly defined and communicated for all those working on the project. Further, there must be a mechanism for project teams to make formal requests to expand the scope. They may not make unilateral changes, or else the project will get completely out of control, but they must have a mechanism by which they can make business case arguments on the merits of their request to expand the scope.

Resources

Needless to say, an SAP implementation project needs the best and brightest a company can find for project teams. However, the team must not be made up entirely of hotshots. There must be some veteran players as well—folks with credibility in the company and who have been around long enough to know and understand the culture.

They must be willing to change the way business gets done, but they must also understand why business is done now the way it is done and able to articulate to the team the difficulties it will encounter making changes. And there is no better advocate for change than the people who created the current systems and processes.

PROJECT EXECUTION AND CONTROL

Milestones are meaningless without a way to monitor progress. Milestones cannot be achieved without a mechanism for conflict resolution. Progress monitoring and conflict resolution are what project managers will spend much of their time on.

Milestones must be measurable and discrete and build toward the end state. The conflict resolution process must be clearly understood and agreed to at the outset. Monitoring must be regular, cross-functional, and based on achieving the milestones determined.

Another large part of project execution is managing expectations. There are four main constituencies for an SAP implementation, and they all have different expectations.

Executives define their expectations by looking at what the ERP solution will provide for the overall business. These expectations have often been created after the executive has been through the SAP sale process and seen demonstrations of all the software's potential bells and whistles.

Executives are highly susceptible to SAP's sales pitch—after all, it is they who are pitched to—and their expectations of the integrated solution, and how it will affect the company, may or may not be realistic. Once this expectation is set in place, it is often hard to change. Program and project managers must know and understand what is realistic and what is not, and need to constantly work to re-adjust executive expectations toward the realistic.

Team members' expectations of the implementation are fraught with personal anxiety. Their heads are spinning with questions such as: What do I get from all this extra effort? Will I have a job here after all this is in place? If so, what will that job be? Can I be promoted from my two years here or is this a dead end? If some of the work is outsourced, will I be outsourced with it? Can I possibly move on as an SAP expert? Can I get more money for this knowledge I am acquiring, either within the company or somewhere else?

Many companies try to guarantee team members employment after the implementation, although with the way work is radically altered by SAP software, that employment may not be doing what the individual previously did. This is where program and project managers take on their counseling and mentoring role.

Key system users ask a set of more functional questions, such as: Will it work? Is it as good as the demo? Why give up what I already have? In the end, their anxieties also show through when they invariably ask: Will the software replace me?

Finally, consultants have expectations also. They are looking for engagements that fit with their personal strengths and goals. More than that, they are looking for engagements that will succeed, for companies that have enough prestige to buff up their own resumes.

Project managers need to go to their management that has the personal relationship with the consulting firm if they sense that the effort is not being supported by the best consulting help possible. Your company should not be the training ground for a bunch of low-level consulting talent that just came out of SAP's partner training school.

Also, if consultants begin to smell failure, the ones that have the experience and the expertise to be in demand for other jobs will bail out of yours. Losing consulting talent can be an early warning that the project is losing its focus or that you are losing control of the project. If the senior or better consultants are turning over more work to the young, inexperienced, and less formidable talent, project managers and the program manager need to get together with the consultant's project manager to find out what is happening.

Finally, there may be times when one must read the riot act to the steering committee to get executive management back into the loop. If executive management commitment has flagged, not even the best program and project management can salvage the effort. Knowing when and how to do this is the greatest asset a project manager can have.

PROGRAM MANAGEMENT

Project management refers to projects involving major elements of SAP implementation. Programs include a number of projects, each of which may have some or no elements of SAP implementation in them.

The keys to program management are alignment and balance. Program managers seek to align the objectives of each individual project with the company's overall objectives. They seek to balance the resources going to individual projects so as to keep all projects on track, achieving deliverables in a relatively uniform fashion.

Remember, the goal of an SAP R/3 implementation program is to create integration of the system across boundaries within the company. If some projects in some departments, functions, or business units are lagging other projects, it is more difficult to achieve this integration.

Finally, program managers are responsible for conflict mediation and resolution as different projects within departments, functions, and business units jostle for resources and work to achieve their objectives.

Alignment of Objectives

What is meant by alignment of objectives? Think of an R/3 implementation across departmental, functional, and business unit lines as an eight-man crew race. The eight rowers in a championship crew are each phenomenally strong and strong willed. They are capable of getting their boat from the beginning of the course to the end of the course no matter how they row.

The biggest and strongest team does not always win, however. It is the team that is most coordinated—most aligned—that gets to the end of the course first.

Think about it. The crew is rowing backward, so they really cannot see where their destination is. In many ways, those involved in each project within an R/3 implementation program are rowing backward also, unable to see where they are going. The program manager acts as the coxswain, calling out in rhythm for the projects to stroke together, making sure there are no obstructions in their way, and keeping an eye on the end of the course, as well as the intermediate milestone markers.

Of course, being program manager for an R/3 implementation is more complex than steering a rowing crew. Crew members have a very simple mission and each individual knows the value of teamwork, but departments, functions, and business units within a company often have more complex and distinct missions. There are different business drivers for each, and the R/3 system has a different impact on each.

The implementation team members, as well as rank and file within each department, function, or business unit, must be educated about the system's dependencies, the value of maintaining common scope and synchronized time lines, and the impact of going it alone. It has been suggested at some companies that each functional area implementing SAP go it alone and meet at the end of the road. We have never seen that approach work.

Resource Allocation and Conflict Resolution

Program managers are most concerned with one central issue: Can all teams achieve their deadlines? To answer this question, program managers must look at whether each team has the necessary resources to succeed in its project. It is their job to allocate often scarce internal business and technical resources, as well as consulting resources, across the spectrum of projects.

Only when resource allocation is done appropriately can each team be asked to achieve the same deliverables on the same time scales, so that the deliverables can be properly integrated into a workable system.

Finally, program managers are responsible for resolving conflicts between the projects. These may take a variety of forms, including time lines, scope, perceived objectives, and limited or restricted resources.

15

Change Management

Change management refers to the effort it takes to manage people through the emotional ups and downs that inevitably occur when an organization is undergoing massive change.

The implementation of SAP software and the business process change that must simultaneously occur necessarily affect a business's organizational structure and, more importantly, the individual roles that a number of people have within the organization.

An active change management approach helps to make a systems implementation project successful by (1) building people's understanding of and commitment to changes associated with the implementation; (2) aligning key organizational elements (structures, roles, and skills) to support the implementation; and (3) enabling continuous improvement to sustain the change.

In surveys seeking to define the key elements of success for major projects, including systems implementations and business process re-engineering, change management is always cited, as is communication, which is seen as an integral part of change management. Carr and Johannson, in their book on best practices in re-engineering, listed communicating the vision and strategies for change as one of those best practices.[1]

Successful change management must provide each and every individual within the organization a sense of ownership in the vision of the "to be." Everyone must understand why the company needs to get from the "as is" to the "to be," and must understand what role they will be asked to play in that future state. At the same time, an organizational structure must be created that enhances how work gets done, and the organization that is in place at the end of the change effort must be more capable of managing future changes.

EASIER TO MANAGE CHANGE DURING GROWTH

Of course, many process redesign exercises and systems implementations will lead to a need for fewer people than under the old way of doing business. In growing businesses, people can be offered the ability to move into other areas.

One financial services company that re-engineered many of the back-office functions in its private banking unit retrained people to perform marketing and product development work,and set up a new group of "middle office" people to act as liaisons between private bankers or their clients and the back-office processes. This, in turn, freed up private bankers from many routine chores, allowing them to find new clients and increase their financial productivity. The end result was that more clients performed more transactions, with better quality and service to the client, with the same number of people in the organization. The company increased its revenues and profit, and more people within the organization had upgraded skill sets, and jobs that paid better and were more challenging.

In companies with flat or declining market share, change management is often more difficult. As individuals realize that fewer people will be needed in the "to-be" state, their willingness to work through the change often wanes. Many times, the most marketable individuals with skills that will be needed after the change head for the lifeboats, while those who fear they may be asked to leave in the "to-be" state dig in their heels and resist the change.

RISKS TO ORGANIZATIONAL CHANGE

There are two broad categories of risks in undertaking organizational change: the validity of decisions made and the effectiveness of the implementation of those decisions. Change management focuses on implemen-

Exhibit 15.1   The Four Change Roles

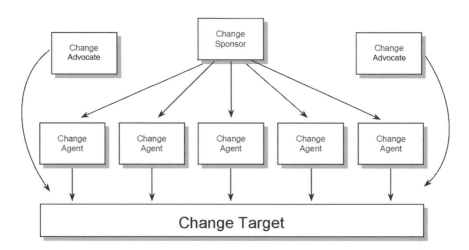

tation and the management of key organizational elements to align them with the desired change.

Successful change management can only occur when the first variable, the validity of decisions, is accepted by all concerned. This means that leadership must create both a burning platform—a reason for why change must occur—and a vision of what the organization will look like after the change occurs.

For a company looking to implement an enterprise resource system, the burning platform can be poor flow of information from production to accounting; aging systems, with rapidly increasing maintenance costs; a merger or divestiture; or any number of other business reasons.

One way to try to mitigate these risks is to define clearly who within the organization falls into each of the four key roles of any change effort. These four roles are shown in Exhibit 15.1.

1. The *change sponsor* is the individual or group who legitimizes the change.
2. The *change agent* is the individual or group responsible for implementing the change.

3. The *change target* is the individual or group who must actually change.

4. The *change advocate* is the individual or group who wants to achieve a change but does not possess the power within the organization to legitimize the effort.

CHANGE MANAGEMENT PROCESS

Change is a process. It is often the largest jeopardy to an SAP implementation project and is easily overlooked. An organization can undergo successful change only if those in the leadership are willing to let the natural process take its course. This process affects every individual in the organization. For some individuals, the change process is a wrenching experience; for others, it is something they embrace.

Exhibit 15.2 shows the change process.

Exhibit 15.2   Change Is a Process

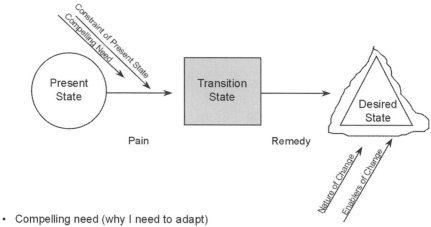

- Compelling need (why I need to adapt)
- Constraint of status quo (what I say is holding me back)
- Pain message (what I have actively listened to and now accept)
- Remedy (the actions I have publicly "signed up" to take)
  –Attitudes>>>>>Intentions>>>>>Behaviors
- Nature of change (what I will experience as I take action)
- Enablers of change (the things that will help me along)

Resistance to Change: Is It Manageable?

What is resistance to change? Is it inevitable? What causes it? How can it be managed?

Recall changes that have affected you, either personally or professionally. Did the experience create stress? Anxiety? Uncertainty? How did you perceive the change? Was it positive and beneficial? Or was it unavoidable, unnecessary, and undesirable?

What determines how changes are perceived? To a large extent, change is viewed in terms of its effects. Will I benefit? Will I be better off as a result of the change? What will need to occur during the change?

Exhibit 15.3 lists some of the characteristics of a negative or a positive response to change.

When the benefits and the payoffs associated with an upcoming change are evident, people "buy in" to the overall direction of the change.

Exhibit 15.3   Characteristics of Response to Change

Negative	Positive
Immobilization	**Uniformed optimism**
· Fearful, confused	· Positive feelings about the change
· Appear overwhelmed	· High confidence in themselves
Denial	**Informed pessimism**
· Defending against a shift	· Negative feelings about the change
· See change as an unacceptable reality	· Low confidence in themselves
Anger	**Hopeful realism**
· Effort to regain control	· Begin to perceive the change project as achievable
· Desire to present stability	· Reduced negative feelings about the change
	· Increase in self-confidence
Bargaining	**Informed optimism**
· Trying to minimize impact	· High levels of positive energy
	· Increased self-confidence brought by the approaching success
Depression	**Completion**
· Frustration	· Strong support of the change
· Sense of loss	· Willingness to help others through the transition
· Low levels of coping	· High self-confidence

Resistance stems from perceived loss—loss of the known and tried and loss of personal choice. Examples of fears held by employees that create resistance to change are job loss or other adverse impact, as well as a shift in communication patterns, organizational structure, influence, authority, and control. Whether the threat is actual or imagined, it should always be treated as real. Reduce fear by removing uncertainties, using education and demonstration.

People resist the imposition of change that is simply ordered to happen without everyone's prior involvement. To minimize resistance, seek involvement of those affected by the change in determining how or if a change should happen. This will lessen the feelings of lost control.

The degree of ease and success with which an organizational change is introduced is directly proportional to the amount of choice that people feel they have in determining and implementing the change. Communicating anticipated changes should incorporate the elements of personal choice, highlighting possible options instead of a singular predetermined path.

It is also possible that people believe the planned change is ill-fated and will not work, or may violate deeply held values and beliefs. This may stem from underlying value differences or intellectual/technical differences in approach and philosophy. The best response is to counter with well-conceived, influential explanations incorporating facts, anecdotal evidence, and data. Conclusions drawn from inadequate data and weak linkages invite opposition.

Encouraging overt resistance is one strategy for identifying and developing responses to individuals experiencing a values conflict. Overtly expressing resistance can help individuals surface and overcome resentments rooted in loss of control. Covert resistance is hazardous to the change project and should be transformed into overt resistance whenever recognized.

Finally, some people resist change because they have a low tolerance for change in general. Provide them with as much reassurance as possible as they move into a world of uncertainty. Time may also reduce anxiety as fears are proven unwarranted.

The key objective is to predict, or at least recognize, resistance; uncover the root cause; and to act directly to minimize or overcome it.

CHANGE MANAGEMENT APPROACH

Our approach to change management has the following five components:

1. Mobilize
2. Assess
3. Plan
4. Implement
5. Renew and sustain

Mobilize

During this phase, the project's scope should be confirmed and the strategy for conducting change management outlined. Change management teams are formed and team leaders chosen. Leaders of process change and system implementation teams, as well as the sponsors of these efforts, are trained in the concepts of change management. Leaders of process change and system implementation teams must be chosen based partly on their ability to be agents of change.

Assess

In this stage, the current human resource situation should be analyzed and the purpose and nature of the change as it affects employees defined. The entire change process (both human and technological changes), as well as its implications for work, must be articulated to the entire organization.

A large part of this assessment is an assessment of the organization's readiness to change. A number of key organizational variables are relevant in a systems implementation.

The impact on the *external environment*, on suppliers, customers, and shareholders must be assessed.

Leadership is necessary to set the direction for the change effort by clearly articulating both the reason the change is necessary (the burning platform) and the vision of how the company will enhance its competitive position through undergoing the change.

Both a *vision* and a *strategy* for change must be clearly articulated and communicated to the entire organization. It is not enough to say, "I have a vision of scoring a touchdown." It is necessary to say, "We're going to run these types of plays, in this order, so we can score a touchdown."

The current *organizational culture* must be congruent with such changes, or it must be willing and able to adapt to the desired changes.

Management practices must foster support and commitment to the change effort.

The *work-unit climate* must be receptive to change.

Finally, the *organizational structure* can be a facilitator or inhibitor of change. Current business process redesign and systems modernization efforts both work on the principle of flattening organizational hierarchy, leaving lean central organizations responsible for overall strategy and some general and administrative functions in a "shared services" environment. Most operating and tactical decision making is left to business unit officers. A rigid, hierarchical structure, with slow and cumbersome decision making at the executive management level, is a great inhibitor to change.

Motivation is a key factor for adopting an improvement.

The *skills* and *abilities* of individuals and the *task requirements* of the R/3 implementation must be matched.

Individual needs and values must not be seen to be contradicted by the project. Areas of congruence should be highlighted to foster support.

There must be clear mechanisms to report on both *individual* and *organizational performance* in relation to the change.

Plan

In this stage, strategies are developed to bridge the gap between the as-is situation and the desired to-be state. This strategy is then translated into tactics for instilling change, including the following:

- o Determination of process and job redesign needs
- o A plan for organizational interventions
- o Development of communications and awareness programs
- o Creation of training curriculum content

Implement

During this stage of change management, understanding of and commitment to change must be built, the staff trained toward the new business goals and organizational outcomes, and new ways of working established.

Both the change plan and the communication plan must be implemented simultaneously. Sponsors, coaches, executives, and team members all have to be aligned in their activities.

Mechanisms must be set up for cross-team learning, and training programs need to be piloted, then rolled out across the organization.

Renew and Sustain

In this final stage, a system of ongoing support for the workforce is developed, as well as a system of measurement to assess the achievement of change and the learning that has occurred. It is possible to tinker with the change plan and redirect it as needed for a second round of organizational change.

Training and education programs should be evaluated and modified as necessary for any future changes. The results of the effort must be communicated. Individuals and groups should be commended for their work and their continuing efforts to enhance the business through achievement of the to-be state.

ORGANIZATIONAL CULTURE AND ITS RELATION TO CHANGE

Organizational culture is the personality of the organization—the collective pattern of beliefs, values, behaviors, and philosophy developed over time. According to the organizational dynamics author and consultant J. Steven Ott, there are five levels of culture that exist within an organization.[2]

1. **Artifacts.**   Artifacts are manifestations of the company's heritage and cultural activity (myths, ceremonies, jargon, and logos). It is important to know what these artifacts mean about the organization.

Exhibit 15.4   The Degree of Consistency of Change

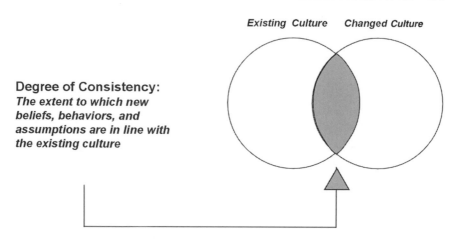

Degree of Consistency:
The extent to which new beliefs, behaviors, and assumptions are in line with the existing culture

2. **Patterns of behavior.**   Patterns of behavior include customs, traditions, habits, and patterns of interaction, such as how decisions are made, what is done to fit and in, and what is needed to get ahead.

3. **Behavioral norms.**   Norms are the house rules, the unwritten but observed code for working. These include beliefs about acceptable and unacceptable behaviors such as cooperation and competition between and among departments, and the behaviors it takes to fit in and to get ahead.

4. **Values.**   Values are the shared beliefs regarding organizational identity and ethics, as seen in corporate ideologies and patterns. Values reflect the priorities assigned to particular behaviors.

5. **Fundamental assumptions.**   Fundamental assumptions are the glue that holds the organization together. They are shared by all, and members live by them.

The odds of successfully implementing change grow as the similarity grows between the existing culture and the behaviors and assumptions required by the change initiative, as well as those behaviors and assumptions that will be part of the desired state, as shown in Exhibit 15.4.

When current culture is in conflict with the necessary culture, the following three options exist for those leading the change effort:

1. Modify the change to be more in line with the existing beliefs, behaviors, and assumptions of the culture.
2. Modify the beliefs, behaviors, and assumptions of the culture to be more supportive of the change.
3. Prepare for the change effort to fail.

The change methods outlined earlier can be used to accomplish either option 1 or option 2, or a combination of those two options.

A FINAL WORD

Too often, an implementation of SAP R/3 software is considered a technical change that has implications only to the information technology (IT) organization. In reality, SAP software affects every function across parts of the organization in which it is implemented, including most notably finance and operations.

It is imperative that program managers, project managers, and team leaders be chosen based as much on their "people skills" as on their technical and business skills.

Handholding each member of the organization through the massive change an Enterprise Resource Planning (ERP) system entails is a big part of all leadership positions in an R/3 implementation.

Notes

1. David K. Carr and Henry J. Johansson, *Best Practices in Reengineering: What Works and What Doesn't in the Reengineering Process* (New York: McGraw-Hill, 1995).

2. J. Steven Ott, *The Organizational Culture Perspective* (Pacific Grove, CA: Brooke Cole Publishing, 1991).

Part III

The Implementor's View: The Implementation Process

This section tackles the implementation process itself. It is not a methodology per se, although it is consistent with our Summit R/3 methodology.

In Chapter 16, our discussion of functionality is expanded. Those who will manage the implementation effort—program managers, project managers, and team leaders—need a more detailed understanding of the R/3 software than executives do.

To describe the level of integration in all its detail would take too long; in fact, books have been written about just that topic. Instead, a series of detailed graphics is presented that will hopefully help people understand how the pieces fit together.

Chapters 17 and 18 deal with the project life cycle as seen through the lens of our Summit R/3 methodology. Chapter 17 deals with the planning and prework, and Chapter 18 discusses the integration, testing, and cut-over from legacy systems to the new SAP system.

Chapter 19 considers the actual structure of the deployment—whether it will occur by business unit, by process, or in a "big bang" across the company and all processes. Chapter 20 follows with a discussion of how to manage the delicate tasks of integration throughout the project life cycle.

Finally, Chapters 21 and 22 expand on the subject of tools, dealing with tools developed by SAP and those developed by third parties to assist with the implementation.

16

Understanding Enough about R/3 Functionality to Drive the Implementation Process

Entire books have been written about a single aspect of SAP R/3 functionality. This chapter is merely meant to give enough understanding to drive the implementation forward.

However, before looking at the functionality provided by SAP software, it is important to understand the underlying structure that ties it all together in a logical manner. This structure is called the enterprise model. It comprises a number of interrelated codes, which are intended to represent the stable entities of a business, such as companies, factories, and physical locations.

Exhibit 16.1 shows the enterprise model codes, listed by major modules.

Each module of SAP has a number of key codes that relate to each other and to the enterprise model codes used by other functional areas. An example is shown in Exhibit 16.2.

The definitions of these codes form a framework on which the business processes are built, and around which variations can be configured into the system. Each code allows certain processes to be defined and to

Exhibit 16.1   Enterprise Model Codes Listed by Major Module

FI	CO/PS	MM	PM	SD	HR
• Company Code • Business Area • Credit Control Area • Financial Management Area	• Operating Concern • Controlling Area	• Plant • Shipping Point • Loading Point • Purchasing Organization • Purchasing Group • MRP Controller • Work Scheduler • Capacity Planner • Plant Storage Area • Storage Location • Warehouse Complex	• Plant Section • Maintenance Planning Plant • Maintenance Planner Group • Maintenance Site Plant • Company Area	• Sales Area Division (Sales) • Sales Organization • Distribution Channel • Sales Office • Sales Group	• Employee Group • Employee Area

vary. For example, company code forms the base on which legal and statutory financial reporting processes are configured.

By defining different company codes, the system can be configured to support entirely different statutory reporting requirements, such as those for different countries or trading blocks. The key point is that the use of these codes and their values must be in place before detailed processes can be built into the system.

Exhibit 16.2   Financial View of Organizational Elements

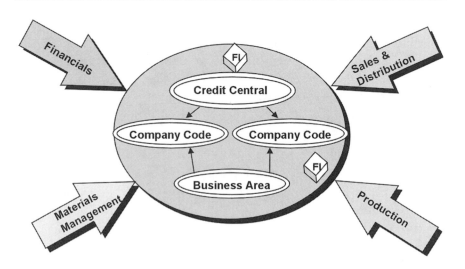

Exhibit 16.3   Controlling View of Organizational Elements

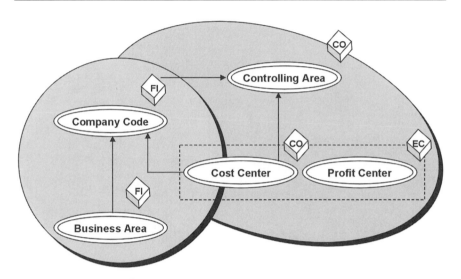

What is critical is that since the configuration tables are keyed on these codes, changes in their use partway through an implementation can mean major changes to configuration and, in the worst case where part of the business is already live with SAP, a reimplementation. Thus, it is best to represent only stable entities with enterprise model codes, defining more flexible business entities as master data records, which can be changed by users on a day-to-day basis in the live system.

This concept appears simple, but can rapidly become complicated when we talk about all the codes affecting a particular SAP module. The picture for finance is relatively straightforward. But as you delve into the other modules it becomes increasingly bewildering, with more and more codes interacting. Exhibits 16.3, 16.4, and 16.5 show how this complexity builds.

The situation becomes overwhelming for anyone approaching the problem as a single issue; the more codes considered, the greater the complexity. Even considering one code at a time can be difficult, when seen from the perspective of looking at the relationships between that one code and the rest of the enterprise model. This is shown in Exhibit 16.6.

This situation is not helped by people who say things like "It depends" or "Well, you could do that, but it affects the controlling areas,

Exhibit 16.4 Sales & Distribution View of Organizational Elements

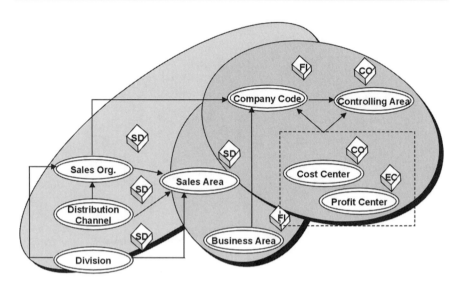

Exhibit 16.5 Materials Management View of Organizational Elements

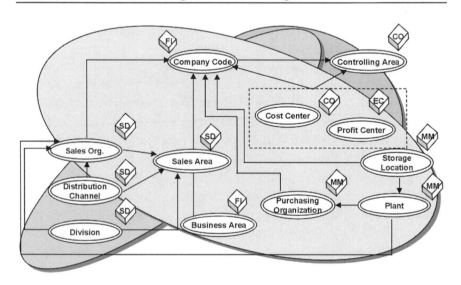

Exhibit 16.6   Plant Code Touch Points

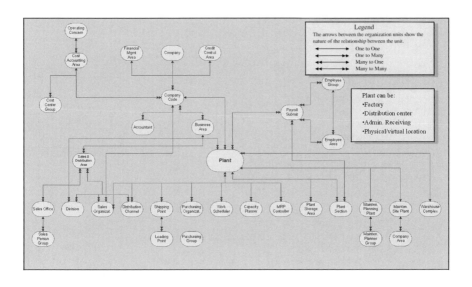

which affects the sales and distribution modules, which feeds back to company code, which affects plant, which touches everything, so you have to be careful. But don't worry, I'll figure it out for you. Oh, and if we get it wrong, you'll only have to start all over again."

The key is: DON'T PANIC![1]

The system was designed to accommodate a wide variety of businesses and local environments. It has a great deal of flexibility. Defining the use of the codes is quick and manageable, as long as you focus on the business, starting with fundamentals, such as statutory books, and what you are trying to achieve, rather than the technical complexity of the system.

By doing this, the problem becomes one of examining the critical business functions, and not highly complex interrelationships. A decision tree such as the one shown in Exhibit 16.7 can be created for each of the major codes, which allows a complex problem to be broken down into a series of simple questions and answers.

As each of the codes falls into place, the number of options for the more detailed codes is reduced, and the decisions become simpler. Indeed, it is this principle that SAP has used for the Business Engineer that makes

Exhibit 16.7   Example or Decision Tree to Decide if a Business Entity Is a Plant

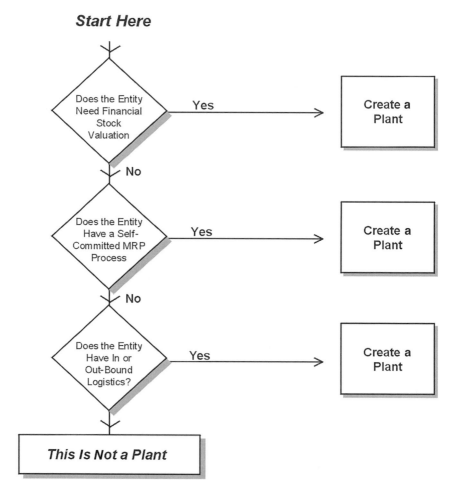

its first appearance in Release 4.0, which asks the questions in the decision tree and guides the user through creating the Enterprise Model. SAP functionality can be divided into the following five areas:

1. **Architecture.**   This supports the system and its development and is mainly the purview of the chief information officer (CIO). This includes Basis and the other common functions.

2. **Finance.** This supports both financial and management accounting and is where the chief financial officer (CFO) uses the system.

3. **Logistics.** This is the part of the system the chief operating officer (COO) is most concerned with, since it supports the entire product pipeline and operations.

4. **Human resources.** This supports personnel issues.

5. **Industry specific.** Increasingly, specific solutions are being designed for particular industries. These specific solution modules tie back to all of the other functional areas: architecture, finance, logistics, and human resources.

ARCHITECTURE

The system architecture includes both technical and business functionality, including the Basis system and the Business Engineering Workbench. SAP's front end has the look and feel of a windows-based system. The functions described here are essentially the first window seen, and one can go layers and layers into the system through the use of pull-down windows. Data can also be loaded from SAP onto many desktop packages.

Within the Basis system is a data dictionary, which defines fields, templates, and elements, and a host of tools used by developers and programmers in customizing SAP to particular uses. These tools include advanced business application programming (ABAP) tools, tools for monitoring the system to see who is doing what at what time on the system, electronic data interchange (EDI) tools, and application link enabling (ALE) tools.

SAP is moving its software increasingly toward distributed architecture. The ALE tools allow you to set up different applications on different pieces of hardware and have a "virtual system" among many boxes. In Release 4.0 these links will be enhanced.

The Business Engineering Workbench is described in detail in the following section on SAP tools.

FINANCE

The finance portion of R/3 is a group of accounting modules designed to meet internal and external accounting requirements. They reflect both the financial and management accounting requirements. They reflect both the financial and management accounting effects of operational business events.

The finance area includes the following modules:

- o FI—financial accounting
- o CO—controlling (management accounting)

Together, these two modules make up what American businesses know as the general ledger.

- o AM—asset management
- o TR—treasury
- o IM—capital investment management
- o EC—enterprise controlling
- o PS—project system

All modules include some common functionality. They are all able to deal with multiple currencies. They are all compliant with generally accepted accounting practices (GAAP). They all provide a clear audit trail, and they all provide reporting.

There is a little glitch that is worth noting with regard to audit and reporting. Since this system can be set up on a global basis, it is important to think when setting the system up about where the time and date stamp will be carried out.

For instance, if Paul enters data at 5:00 P.M. in Milan and Ralph at 2:00 P.M. in New Jersey, Ralph's entry is actually being made later than Paul's. If the system is designed to time and date stamp for each person's local time, it would be impossible to conduct a proper activity audit. To get around this, most companies choose to time and date stamp material with either the local time of world headquarters or with Greenwich Mean Time, for example.

Exhibit 16.8   SAP Coding Block Principles

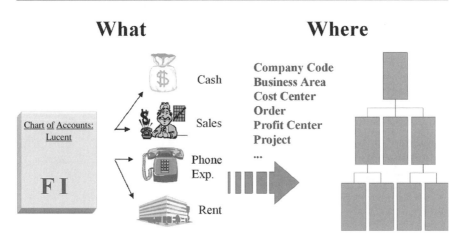

Financial Accounting

The FI module provides an external view of a company's financial activities only, providing profit and loss, balance sheet, and cash flow information. All other management accounting information resides in the CO module.

This can be thought of as dividing the posting of SAP financial documents into "what" the posting is and "where" in the organization it is posted, as shown in Exhibit 16.8.

The FI module supports statutory requirements for a variety of countries, including the United States and all European Union (EU) members. It supports multicurrency functionality and is compliant with the European Monetary Union (EMU).

Exhibit 16.9 shows the main links into and out of the FI modules with the other modules in the finance areas.

The FI module contains comprehensive accounts receivable tools and provides tight integration of accounts receivable and accounts payable with sales and purchasing.

The module does multinational consolidations and integrates with treasury and cash management. It provides simultaneous updates with other modules, including management accounting.

Exhibit 16.9   Main Links to Fl

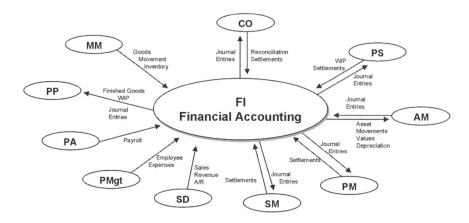

The following are major subdivisions of the FI module:

o FI-GL—general ledger
o FI-SL—special ledgers
o FI-AR—accounts receivable
o FI-AP—accounts payable
o FI-LC—legal consolidation
o FI-FA—financial asset management

Controlling

The CO module provides management accounting functionality and an internal view of the business. The module is integrated very tightly with other SAP modules, especially FI. Some accounts are shared with FI.

Management accounting can cross legal entities, and allocations can be made across legal entities without hitting financial accounts. The module provides flexible tools for cost planning and analysis.

Exhibit 16.10 shows the linkages to and from the CO module with other R/3 modules.

This module supports most modern cost accounting methods, including activity-based costing, actual costing, static and flexible normal or standard costing, activities and service costing, and functional costing.

Exhibit 16.10   Main Links to CO

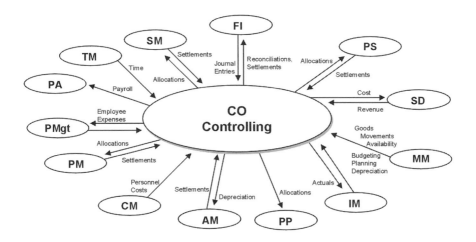

The following are submodules of the controlling module:

- ○ CO-CCA—cost center accounting
- ○ CO-ABC—activity-based costing
- ○ CO-OPA—order and project accounting
- ○ CO-PC—product costing
- ○ CO-PA—profitability analysis
- ○ CO-PCA—profit center accounting

Asset Management

The AM module tracks hard assets. Key features of the module include financial management of assets for life-cycle management, and integration with plant maintenance (PM) for full asset management. The module keeps multiple books for financial, tax, and depreciation recording.

Exhibit 16.11 shows the main links in and out of the AM module.

Treasury

Treasury is one of the newer modules in the SAP repertoire and is a key module. It is used for managing liquidity, financial assets, and risks. The

Exhibit 16.11   Main Links to AM

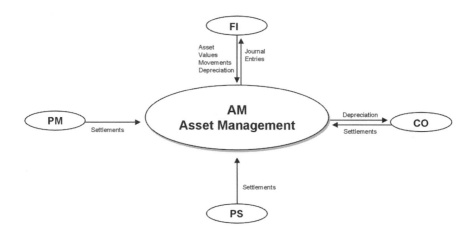

TR module supports trading and settlement activities, including money markets, foreign exchange, securities, derivatives, and loans. It also performs market risk analysis. All of this is done with real-time data.

Exhibit 16.12 shows the linkages into and out of the TR module.

The following are major components of the treasury module:

- o TR-CM—cash management
- o TR-FM—funds management
- o TR-TM—treasury management

Exhibit 16.12   Main Links to TR

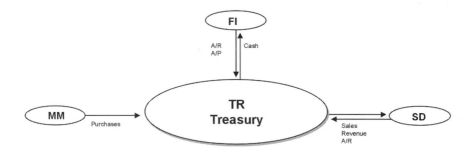

Capital Investment Management

The IM module supports the capital investment and budgeting process, and can be pulled down to deal with capital investments needed for individual projects. It monitors both internal costs and external acquisitions.

The module provides for cross-company budgeting, as well as for program budgeting and analysis of budget versus actual expenditures. It integrates tightly with other financial modules.

Exhibit 16.13 shows the links between IM and other modules.

Submodules of IM include the following:

o IM-FA—tangible fixed assets
o IM-FI—Financial investments (This is actually more of a treasury submodule, but resides here. It provides the same functionality as does the treasury management submodule of the treasury module.)

Enterprise Controlling

The EC module does not really link to other modules. It provides little stand-alone functionality, but acts as a "roll up" module, pulling data from all financial modules.

Enterprise controlling shares much functionality with the control module, reporting data gathered from CO, as well as from the FI module, and the human resources and logistics areas.

Project System

The PS module sits in both the finance and logistics areas. It provides for full project management, including networks and critical paths. It supports a wide variety of business projects and can link external projects to sales and distribution.

The module provides for milestone billing and capacity planning and management. It tracks relationships and can be used to perform critical path analysis.

Exhibit 16.13   Main Links to IM

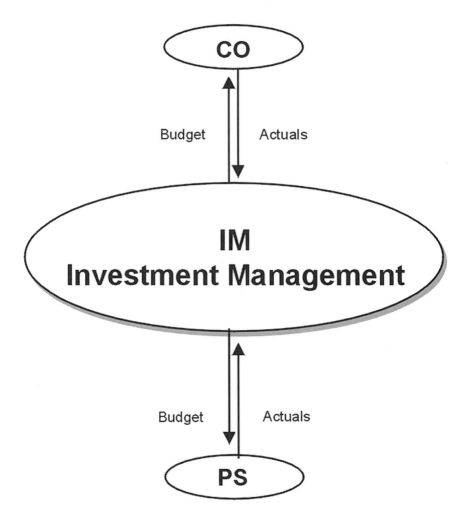

Exhibit 16.14 shows the links into and out of the project system module.

This module supports a wide variety of projects, including the following:

o Research and development (R&D)
o Engineer to order

Exhibit 16.14   Main Links to PS

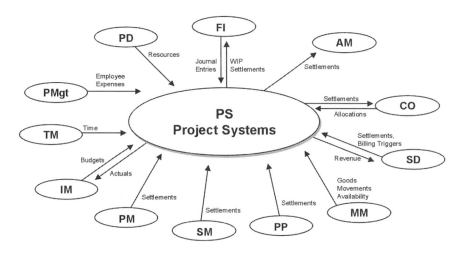

- o Investment programs (asset construction)
- o Construction
- o Data processing
- o Government
- o Service-based

LOGISTICS

This group of modules provides support for inbound and outbound logistics, as well as a variety of different manufacturing environments, including discrete, make-to-stock, and make-to-order. There are a number of bolt-on software packages that add functionality, such as computer-aided design (CAD) and mobile data entry.

Logistics includes operations from requisition of materials until the goods are delivered and the bill is sent. The following are modules within this area of functionality:

- o MM—materials management (This is perhaps the largest module in the entire SAP system.)
- o PP—production planning
- o PM—plant maintenance

o QM—quality management
o SD—sales and distribution
o SM—service management

Materials Management

The MM module is designed to optimize the purchasing process, using work flow, vendor evaluation, inventory, and warehouse management.

Key features of the MM module include purchasing of both goods and services, inventory management, warehouse management, transportation, invoice verification, sales and operations planning, and ALE for central procurement contracts.

Materials management is the key to being able to produce what the customer needs, when it is needed. Information regarding customer orders, from the sales and distribution (SD) module, automatically move into the materials management module, so that you can acquire the right materials to perform the customer order.

Purchase requisitions from anywhere in the company move automatically to purchasing, where they are converted into purchase orders. Buyers can compare prices, automate vendor selection for certain items, or automate order creation where vendors are preselected.

Exhibit 16.15 shows the major links into and out of the MM module. The following are MM's major submodules:

o MM-MRP—materials requirement planning
o MM-PUR—purchasing
o MM-IM—inventory management
o MM-WM—warehouse management
o MM-IV—invoice verification
o MM-IS—information system
o MM-EDI—electronic data interchange

The inventory management (IM) submodule supports receipts, issues, and stock transfers, and allows such special stocks as consignment

Exhibit 16.15   Main Links to MM

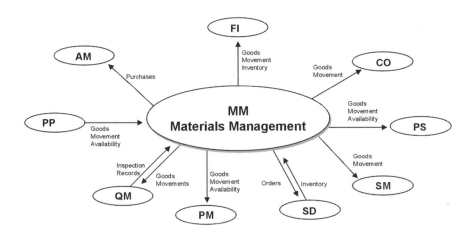

stocks, project stock, returnable packaging, or the company's components to be managed at a subcontractor location.

The warehouse management (WM) submodule allows optimization of material flow by putting away stock in the most available location for future picking, and enables maintenance of a record of all current materials. The submodule works with hand-held terminals, bar-code scanners, and other automated warehouse tools.

An evaluated receipt settlement (ERS) functionality makes it possible to move to an invoiceless purchasing process. The system creates periodic "invoice" reports based on the goods receipts posted in the system, doing away with invoice/purchase order reconciliations.

Production Planning

The PP module supports a variety of production environments. It provides manufacturing and production control, mapping out what machines any material must go through. It works in repetitive manufacturing, make-to-order, make-to-stock, and assemble-to-order environments. It provides for extended MRP II and kanban-type operations.

Exhibit 16.16 shows the links into and out of the PP module.

Exhibit 16.16   Main Links to PP

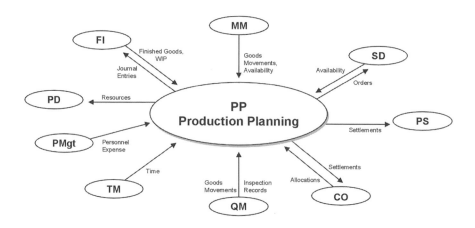

The following are submodules of PP:

○ PP-BD—basic data for production
○ PP-SAP—sales and operations planning
○ PP-MP—master planning
○ PP-MRP—materials requirements planning
○ PP-CRP—capacity requirements planning
○ PP-SFC—production orders
○ PP-PC—product costing

Plant Maintenance

The PM module provides planning, control, and processing of scheduled and unscheduled maintenace. It provides for field service management as well as in-plant management, maintains equipment maintenance histories, and is tightly integrated with the PS, MM, and HR (human resources) modules.

Exhibit 16.17 shows the links in and out of the PM module.

The following are submodules of PM:

○ PM-EQM—equipment and technical objects (sets up what the equipment is)

Exhibit 16.17   Main Links to PM

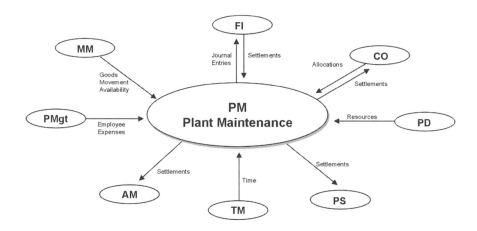

o PM-PRM—preventive maintenance (maintenance plans)
o PM-WOC—maintenance order management (processes to prevent or respond to breakdowns)
o PM-PRO—maintenance projects (large-scale programs such as total plant shutdown for overhaul of manufacturing line)
o PM-SMA—sector management
o PM-IS—information systems

Quality Management

Quality management is a small module. It works to manage quality assurance (QA) along the supply chain, integrating quality inspections with production and managing QA-related costs. The module records defects and exchanges data with external systems via e-mail to suppliers and vendors. The module also manages quality notifications and uses work flow to route notification actions.

The QM module is tightly integrated with production modules and includes quality inspection, computer-aided process planning (CAPP), data on tolerances, and specific inspection plans for customers or group plans for a group of parts.

Exhibit 16.18 shows the links into and out of the QM module.

Exhibit 16.18   Main Links to QM

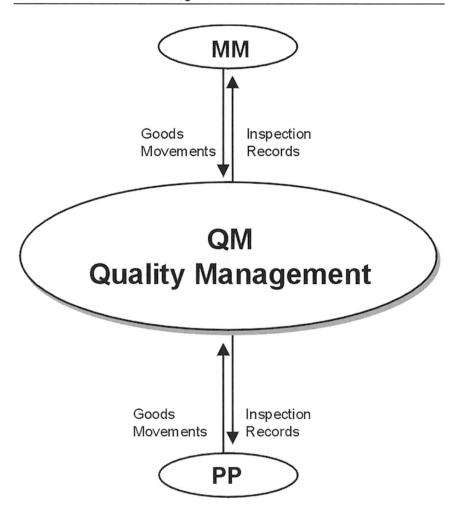

Quality management includes the following major submodules:

- o QM-QP—quality planning
- o QM-QI—quality inspection
- o QM-QC—quality control

- QM-QNC—quality notification and certification
- QM-QMIS—quality management information system

Sales and Distribution

The SD module tracks activities from the receipt of a request for qualifications (RFQ) to billing and shipping product. It provides order cycle processing, including the following:

- Sales and operations planning
- Sales management
- Billing management
- Contract management
- Batch-order processing
- Assembly-order processing
- Transportation
- Export controls

The module is integrated tightly to other logistics modules, as well as to finance modules.

Exhibit 16.19 shows the links into and out of the SD module.

Major submodules of SD include the following:

- SD-MD—master data
- SD-CAS—sales support
- SD-SLS—sales
- SD-SHP—shipping
- SD-BIL—billing

The SD module provides highly automated order entry and pricing, quoting from price lists or customer agreements including any pre-arranged discounts; from product, product group, or product cost; or from sales deals

Exhibit 16.19   Main Links to SD

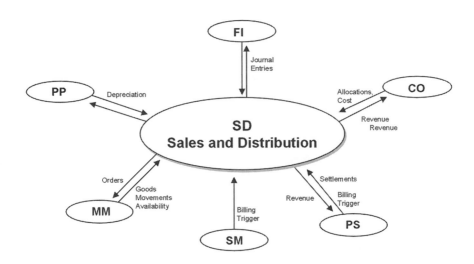

and promotions. The system also carries out a dynamic credit check, and notifies you if the customer fails the check.

Because the system integrates so tightly between SD, MM, and PP, you can verify for your customer at the time of order the availability on the requested delivery date. This kind of window on the entire order pipeline allows for much more effective management of all resources necessary to produce goods.

If there is not availability from your production facility of choice, the system can consolidate availability from many sites. If there is not enough availability, the system can automatically calculate from materials management and production planning information when there will be sufficient product available to meet the particular order.

The SD module integrates picking, packing, and shipping with transportation options, including forwarding agents. It even provides this for foreign trade processing, determining whether particular products can be shipped to specific countries, or to a specific customer. All necessary customs forms are handled automatically.

Billing is automated, with bills sent for orders delivered. Billing documents can be sent by mail, fax, or EDI. Revenue and receivables are immediately visible in the FI and CO components.

Exhibit 16.20   Service Management

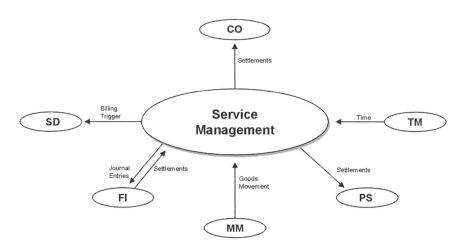

Service Management

The SM module provides an integrated solution for providing service contracts and warranty coverage for customers, billing for service orders, and proper reporting of service information.

Exhibit 16.20 shows the major links to other modules.

The major submodules of the SM module include the following:

- o SM-IBM—installed base management
- o SM-SA—service agreements
- o SM-CM—call management
- o SM-BI—billing and invoicing
- o SM-SIS—service information system

HUMAN RESOURCES

The human resources (HR) area of SAP is a rapidly expanding area of R/3 functionality, which supports a business in its human resource planning, development, and compensation functions. It is composed of the following five modules:

o PMgt—personnel management

o PA—payroll accounting

o OM—organization management

o TM—time management

o PD—personnel development

Personnel Management

The PMgt module provides in an integrated structure a database of personnel who are employed or contracted to the business. It also provides functionality for maintaining the salary and benefit structures available within the business; planning and recruiting for the business; and processing travel and living expenses. Exhibit 16.21 shows the main links between PMgt and other SAP modules.

The following are major submodules of personnel management:

o PMgt-PA—personnel administration

o PMgt-RM—recruitment management

Exhibit 16.21   Main Links to PMgt

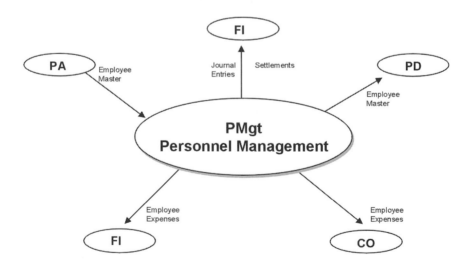

- PMgt-TM—travel management
- PMgt-BA—benefits administration
- PMgt-SA—salary administration

Payroll Accounting

The PA module supports payroll for a wide variety of individual national requirements, including those of the United States and all EU countries. This list expands with each new release of the software. It creates a full trail of all payroll transactions and supports the payment of expenses as well as payroll liabilities. It also allows a business to centralize or decentralize its payroll function based on country or legal entities.

The major links between the PA module and other modules are shown in Exhibit 16.22.

Exhibit 16.22   Main Links to PA

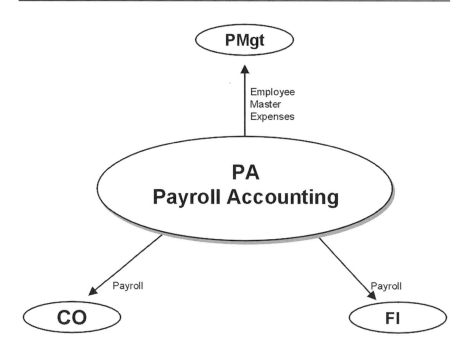

Organization Management

The OM module provides functionality to maintain an accurate picture of the busienss organization with flexibility to change rapidly in order to support a new business environment. The module also supports the planning of personnel costs to ensure that any new organization structures are based on prudent costing, using simulated, planned, or actual payroll figures.

The main links between the OM module and other modules are seen in Exhibit 16.23.

The following are two major submodules of the OM module:

- o OM-OM—organization management
- o OM-PCP—personnel cost planning

Time Management

The TM module supports planning, recording, and controlling time, including shift planning, time exception reporting (e.g., for sick time or vacation), and time reporting for cost allocation where staff charge their time to specific cost objects such as projects or service orders. The major links to time management are shown in Exhibit 16.24.

Time management is divided into the following two major submodules:

- o TM-TM—time management
- o TM-SP—shift planning

Personnel Development

The PD module provides functionality to support the development of individual employees within the business's overall HR structure. It allows individual qualifications and requirements to be recorded and used as part of resource planning, for example, for specific roles on a customer-facing project. The module also supports career and succession planning and the coordination of training programs and business events.

Exhibit 16.23   Main Links to OM

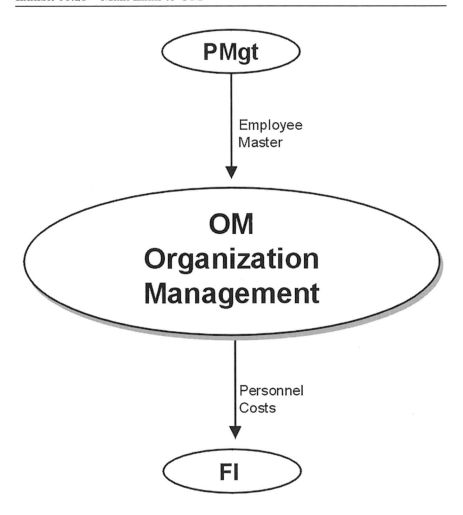

The major links between PD and other modules are seen in Exhibit 16.25.

The following are major submodules in personnel development:

o PD-PD—personnel development
o PD-TCM—training and career management

Exhibit 16.24 Main Links to Time Management

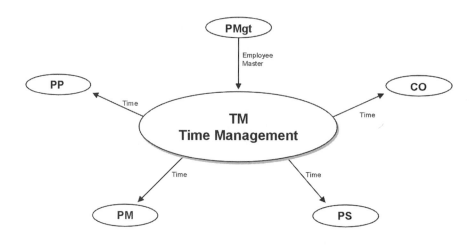

Exhibit 16.25 Main Links to PD

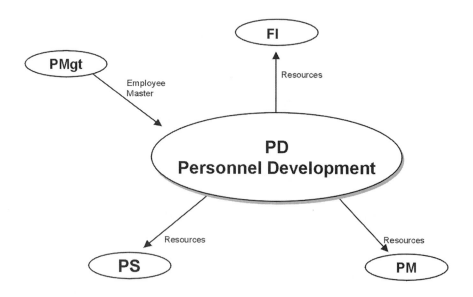

INDUSTRY SPECIFIC

SAP is continually developing more industry-specific modules, which it calls industry solutions. These are enhancements to the standard system that address key issues within a particular industry. They are often developed in conjunction with customers and consulting partners with strength in a particular industry.

The following industry solutions are available today:

o Aerospace and defense
o Automotive
o Banking
o Chemicals
o Consumer products
o Engineering and construction
o Health care
o High tech and electronics
o Insurance
o Oil and gas
o Pharmaceuticals
o Public sector
o Retail
o Telecommunications
o Utilities

Aerospace and Defense

This industry-specific solution concentrates on defense-specific processes such as business acquisition, program management, integrated product and process design, and maintenance repaid and overhaul (MRO). The level of integration within R/3 allows aerospace and defense companies to link enterprise management with core business processes and complementary software. The software has a flexible architecture, which enables each company to tailor the system to meet its particular specifications.

Automotive

SAP's automotive module allows automotive companies to integrate their business infrastructure into a customer-pulled supply chain to form a global selected network of original equipment manufactures (OEMs), tiered system and component suppliers, and the aftermarket. This helps automotive manufacturers become more flexible, innovative, and efficient in order to reduce development cycles, production, and order-to-deliver times.

Banking

Changes in the nature of banking are causing a shift in the management emphasis from management of transaction-oriented systems to networked information systems. SAP's banking module allows financial institutions to unify the enormous volume of financial data generated from all of its operations and create consistent information from that data. Banks can build their own information technology (IT) infrastructure with flexibility and the ability to monitor their own particular key performance indicators.

Chemicals

The chemicals module allows a company to integrate its enterprise management, extended supply chain, and plant-specific business processes. R/3 software easily supports process manufacturing, quality management, process costing, and batch/lot management, as well as the management of dangerous substances. The software is based on industry best practices and has the flexibility to allow each chemical company to tailor the system to business and even specific plant needs.

Consumer Products

SAP's consumer products module, together with the company's basic R/3 infrastructure, can help consumer products companies undertake an efficient consumer response (ECR) strategy. It helps minimize costs and maximize efficiencies throughout the supply chain, from procurement to sales. The links between SD, PP, MM, and FI allow a company to see just where profits are generated.

Engineering and Construction

Release 4.0 provides much new functionality for this module. Product data management (PDM) helps with engineering-change management, linking external objects such as documents and drawings among a number of third parties. Cash-flow management assists the controller in day-to-day tracking earned value analysis and profit analysis forecasts. Project simulation allows "what-if" analysis from project beginning through the entire project life cycle. SAP Release 4.0 has an enhanced interface to exchange project data with external systems, such as those of customers and suppliers.

Health Care

The health care module focuses on integrating business processes and people, in order to create more seamless services for patients. Minimized waiting and treatment time not only provides better patient care, but also increases efficiency and lowers cost.

High Tech and Electronics

Timely, accurate, and accessible information is paramount in a high-technology manufacturing environment, as companies compete in a volatile marketplace with little customer loyalty. Global manufacturing and complex logistics, with transfer pricing of components and subassemblies complicates matters. SAP software assists a high-tech company to balance between value pricing and cutting-edge technology to meet the demands of the marketplace.

Insurance

The insurance industry solution, combined with the basic R/3 functionality, allows insurance companies to consolidate data currently held in a multitude of systems. Many insurance companies have traditionally maintained different databases on different systems—one for general ledger accounting, another for regulatory compliance, another for claims, and yet another for expense administration. Enterprise-wide data can now be maintained and used to create consistent information for administrators, managers, and agents.

Oil and Gas

Industry Solution-Oil (IS-Oil) provides a comprehensive accounting system capable of handling many ledgers—legal and regulatory—and providing a global financial snapshot of the company. The oil and gas module combines the basic R/3 architecture with two specific modules, IS-Oil Upstream and IS-Oil Downstream. The Upstream module's key feature is the ability to perform joint venture accounting, supporting cost allocation among joint venture partners while reducing staff overhead and data redundancy. The Downstream module's key feature extends SAP's software to address numerous functions unique to marketing and refining, such as exchange transactions, order fulfillment, hydrocarbon inventory management, and retail management.

Pharmaceuticals

The pharmaceutical module combines with the basic R/3 architecture to assist pharmaceutical companies with operational flexibility, unfailing product quality and consistency, and better time-to-market for research and development (R&D) and new products. The software's components support pharmaceutical-specific issues such as process manufacturing, quality management, and process costing.

Public Sector

The philosophy of public sector management has shifted from one of administering public agencies to one of providing services to clients of the public sector. This means a need for resource management and service costing. The public sector module, in conjunction with basic R/3 architecture, helps public sector entities integrate processes that apply the best features of effective business management, such as active financial management, refined cost management, and efficient personnel management. Many administrative processes can be automated because basic data is entered once into the system, then courses its way to all other areas within the system where it may be accessed.

Retail

Having IT that supports efficient supply chain management is not enough in the retail industry. This must be combined with point-of-sale information about what was bought by a customer, when it was purchased, and where, and as much information as possible about that customer. The retail module allows businesses to monitor the impact of promotions and markdowns, trends, weather, and outside events. It can even be used to analyze demographics and lifestyles.

Telecommunications

The telecommunications module is a solution for telecoms companies of all sizes, with flexibility to allow companies to tailor the system to their own needs. The module takes advantage of R/3's multicompany and multinational functionality, including multilingual and currency-conversion capabilities.

Utilities

The utilities module works with the R/3 architecture to provide utility companies with ways to collect data and create from that data meaningful information with which to compete in the changing world of deregulation, competition, globalization, and increasing customer orientation. The software supports utility-specific processes such as generation, transmission, distributions, and customer service.

17

Initiation and Planning

Recall that in Chapter 8 we briefly discussed our methodology for SAP R/3 implementation, Summit R/3. Summit R/3 has the following seven discrete phases, or modules:

1. Initiation
2. Strategy Analysis
3. Process Design
4. Prototype
5. Develop
6. Transition
7. Sustain

As you move through these seven phases, there are also some continuous activities, integration management, knowledge transfer, technical architecture, performance measurement, project management, and change management.

Rather than dedicate an entire chapter to each of the methodology's modules, we will give you an overview of the methodology in two chapters. This chapter discusses the first three methodology modules—initiation, strategy analysis, and process design—which we believe constitute the planning part of an SAP R/3 implementation. Chapter 18 will deal with the final four modules—prototype, develop, transition, and sustain.

Throughout this implementation process, you will most likely be working with one or more consulting partners. Your roles and responsibilities, as well as those of consulting partners, and the relationship you maintain, are discussed in more detail in Chapter 9.

PROJECT INITIATION

Exhibit 17.1 shows the key tasks and deliverables for this phase in the implementation, as well as the tools and techniques used to successfully complete the phase.

This stage of the implementation process entails confirming the business strategy, establishing the scope of work to be done, and creating a work plan for the implementation. The project management structure is put in place during this phase. Finally, leadership commitment to the project is solicited and cemented. Only if these issues are dealt with can there be a focused R/3 implementation project.

Defining the scope means defining the processes that will undergo redesign in light of R/3, and what the expected usage patterns are for the software. Metrics for the processes are defined, with improvement targets and interim goals set. Budget and resource requirements are established. Constraints, such as legacy systems, are identified.

In order to define the scope, you need to do interviews and conduct workshops with executives, process leaders/owners, and information systems personnel. When the statement of scope is created, it must be agreed to and endorsed by executives, then communicated to the entire organization.

Creating a project management structure involves creating a project organization, which is generally done by process, or by SAP function definitions. Also, a steering committee is necessary. Members of the steering committee should be leaders, key stake holders, a project sponsor, and a funder.

Teams must be created. Some team members must be full time to perform the work. These people should be among the organization's "best

Exhibit 17.1   Project Initiation

Tasks	Key Deliverables	Tools & Techniques

• Scope
• Structure
• Plan
	• Project Announcement Letter
	• Statement of Scope
	• Project Infrastructure
	• Training Plan
	• Project Work Assignments
	• Quality & Change
	  Management Procedures
		• Executive
		  Workshops
		• Summit R/3
		  Estimating
		  Guidelines

and brightest." The team also needs some part-time members to provide input, review, and agreement. Part-time members need detailed knowledge of the various business processes in their "as-is" state.

The team needs to undergo training, both in SAP tools and techniques, as well as in change management and small-group dynamics.

Standards must be developed for the project. These standards ensure that documentation created, as well as tools and techniques used, are uniform and not ad hoc.

At this point, the project structure must be documented and general agreement to the structure obtained.

A project plan is the end stage of all this effort. The plan provides a high-level look at the implementation effort. The plan describes the approach that will be taken—the amount of process re-engineering, the interfaces and conversions that will be necessary, and whether the effort will try to proceed on a fast track or will go more slowly.

Within the overall plan is a more detailed plan for the design phase of the work.

The entire plan should be published for comment, and the project team and steering committee need one more opportunity to look at input from those who comment before moving forward with the plan. After the steering committee walks through the scope, plan, and project structure, it can ask company executives for authorization to proceed.

STRATEGY ANALYSIS

Exhibit 17.2 shows the tasks and deliverables for the phase of work, as well as the tools and techniques used.

The purpose of the strategy analysis module is to analyze the current business and information technology (IT) strategies and supporting core business processes and, assuming that there will be an SAP R/3 implementation, on the organization's business drivers, goals, and objectives.

The strategy analysis allows you to perform a strategic analysis of your organization and ensure that SAP R/3 supports business processes that provide competitive advantage. The following are key strategic questions:

- o What is critical to your business for competitive advantage and regulatory compliance?
- o What plans and management controls exist to address these critical goals?
- o What are your core business processes and their process flows and related performance measures?
- o How will IT support each process, and how has SAP functionality been mapped to satisfy this?
- o How will external and internal performance measures be used to demonstrate the success of your SAP project?

Exhibit 17.2   Strategy Analysis

Tasks	Key Deliverables	Tools & Techniques
• Current Strategy • Future Strategy • SAP Validation • Conceptual Design	• Current Business & IT Strategies • Business Drivers, Goals & Objectives • Core Business Process Scripts • Business Analysis • GAP Analysis	• Workshops • Process Modeling • Customer, Environmental & Competitor Analysis • Summit R/3 Analyzer

In this module you unify your vision for both information systems (IS) and business strategies. The IS and business strategies should be complementary. The level of business change—refinement or radical redesign—is clearly determined. How SAP R/3 fits all of this is defined.

Once the vision is established, you can focus that vision by getting to the next level of detail. Business drivers, goals, and objectives are clearly stated. This allows you to determine the scope of change and, more important, the timetables under which this change should occur. Finally, you look at *how* to change and not just at what to change.

The final bit of the strategy stage is clarifying. Here you do a cost/benefit analysis, finalize the design as to whether to try a fast-track implementation, define the role of your consultants, do risk assessment, and analyze the gaps between the as-is and the to-be to see just how much work there really is.

PROCESS DESIGN

Tasks and key deliverables of the process design phase, as well as the tools and techniques you use to perform those tasks and reach those deliverables, are shown in Exhibit 17.3.

The purpose of the process design module is to target and redesign business processes based on SAP functionality so that they work more

Exhibit 17.3   Process Design

Tasks	Key Deliverables	Tools & Techniques
• Confirm & Target Processes • Redesign Processes • Refine Organization	• Reengineered Business Processes • Process Performance Targets • SAP Business Model • New Organization Structure • Change Management Procedures	• Cost/Benefit Analysis • Process Investment Analysis • Redesign Workshops • R/3 Analyzer

effectively and efficiently. This enables the organization to meet its business strategy objectives.

This phase of work covers process design, interface and conversion design, organizational design, and conceptual design of R/3. This phase results in a working design of SAP R/3 usage throughout the enterprise.

Before you can redesign processes, you need to confirm and document the current processes. You should rank order processes for analysis, with those that contribute most to competitive advantage or those that are "must do's" because of regulatory issues coming first. After studying best practices from other companies, you can analyze and design improvement for your high-priority processes.

The decision of which processes to focus on redesigning leads to the current information systems that support these processes. As part of your process redesign, you determine the information you need to run the process at peak effectiveness. From this, you determine where you need SAP R/3's functionality.

Once you've established which of your data needs R/3 can provide, you can determine which of your current systems can be turned off once R/3 is operational and which ones need to remain as legacy systems. You will need to design interfaces between legacy systems and R/3 and conversions from systems that are being decommissioned to R/3 so you do not lose any historical data.

At this point in the implementation process, it is still acceptable to modify the scope slightly, to "tweak" it where necessary.

As you redesign processes, you will, of necessity, also redesign the organization. A new business process needs an improved organization structure. To do this, you need some assistance and expertise from your colleagues in human resources.

It is imperative that impact on jobs be determined, and that any unions be brought on board early in the process of redefining job roles and rewriting job descriptions. This is a very sensitive area, and constant communication with the steering committee is imperative during this period of time. In addition, the steering committee should probably go back to executive management and reconfirm the authorization to proceed.

Now you are ready to do your conceptual design of the SAP R/3 system. From a picture of expected usage merge new processes, restructured

216

organization, and knowledge of the existing system to design, document, and fully understand (at a high level) how your business will work within an SAP environment.

START RIGHT

A project that starts right finishes right. It is remarkable that many organizations set out to implement SAP without fully understanding why they have purchased the software, how much it will really cost to install, who (operators, customers, suppliers, or shareholders) will actually benefit, and what will change.

Our advice is to start right. The initiation stage of an SAP project is the time to ensure that fundamental questions are answered, that answers are understood by the key people in the organization, and that the project team heads off in the right direction. Shortcuts can cause long delays.

18

Getting SAP in Place

Now that you have taken your SAP R/3 implementation through the phases of matching your information technology (IT) and business strategies, understanding the enterprise model, and re-engineering your business processes, it is time to do the technical work of R/3 implementation. The following are the four phases involved in this work:

1. Prototype
2. Develop
3. Transition
4. Sustain

PROTOTYPE

The purpose of the prototype module is to configure the SAP R/3 system to reflect the organizational structure depicted in the targeted process vision produced in the process design module. Exhibit 18.1 shows the tasks and key deliverables in this module and the tools and techniques used.

This stage of work, sometimes called configuring, includes establishing the customization needed for R/3, configuring the system itself, and testing the system. The end result is a system prototype being built and tested.

To establish the customization needed, there is a need to perform a fit/gap analysis of the business needs against SAP's capability to deliver. The customization needed includes custom programs, as well as specifying and registering modifications to R/3.

There is also a need to confirm the process flow and define the reporting structure for data coming off the system.

Configuring the system includes establishing the SAP Enterprise Model, as well as the master data and mechanisms for sharing in multiple SAP systems. During this part of the effort, there is a need to agree to common items/elements of configuration and perform the configuration.

What exactly is meant by this?

The common elements within SAP software are often referred to as hierarchical elements. The more the software is to be used as an enterprise solution, the more common these elements need to be. The following are examples:

- o Company code
- o Business area
- o Profit center
- o Plant
- o Customer master

Exhibit 18.1   Prototype

Tasks	Key Deliverables	Tools & Techniques
• Customize • Specify Interfaces • Review & Finalize	• System Definition • Reporting Structure • Customized SAP R/3 System • Interface, Data Conversion & System Modifications Specifications • Confirmed Process Flow & Reporting Structure • Transition Plan	• SAP Development Tools • SAP-IMG • C&L Addendum • SAP R/3 System • Workshops

o Vendor master

o Sales area

Configuration means setting up the tables within the SAP software to establish these elements and the business rules around them. Two common "show stoppers" to the configuration process are the inability to agree on business rules, such as transfer pricing and inventory ownership.

Finally, you must test the customization, the individual SAP R/3 functions, and the integration of the entire R/3 system, and when the testing is complete begin working on a transition plan.

DEVELOP

The purpose of the develop module is to develop a correctly performing system, with all required business functions, operational procedures, and interfaces between software and hardware. Also involved are properly performed integration and acceptance tests. Exhibit 18.2 shows the tasks and key deliverables for this module, as well as the tools and techniques used.

This stage of work includes creation of business scripts, system documentation, custom programming, and integration testing. The results are user procedures, training material, finalized interfaces and data conversion programs, and any other custom programs.

Exhibit 18.2   Develop

Tasks	Key Deliverables	Tools & Techniques
• User Procedures • New Module Development • Operations Procedures • Integrated Testing	• Tested and Accepted System • User Procedures • Enhancement Modules • Conversion Modules • Interface Modules • Operations Procedures	• User Procedures Guidelines • SAP Documentation System • IMG/Hypertext • C&L SAP Addendum • SAP Development Tools

Documentation includes both user and operations procedures, as well as user training documentation. Custom programming includes the interfaces and conversions identified in the design phase, as well as any other custom programming determined in the prototype phase.

The final step in this module is to perform integration testing. This includes several tests of the end-to-end process—for instance, a requisition-to-receipt process—to evaluate the system functionality.

TRANSITION

Transition covers the technical aspects of deployment. Management aspects of deployment are discussed in Chapter 19.

The purpose of the transition module is to ensure the successful implementation of the SAP R/3 system into the organization by converting all data, mobilizing the SAP support teams, and transferring accountability to user management. Exhibit 18.3 shows the task and key deliverables for this phase of work as well as the tools and techniques used.

This stage of work covers establishing the R/3 environment, executing the conversions and interfaces, training users, assessing the readiness to move to production, and, finally, instituting a production environment. The outcome is a live SAP R/3 site or multiple SAP R/3 sites.

Establishing the SAP environment means creating the production SAP system, based on the prototyping effort. Conversions from legacy systems being decommissioned are put in place and those systems turned off. Interfaces to legacy systems that will remain are in place. Electronic data transfer links to customers, suppliers, and others are in place. Other software has been custom generated or purchased and "bolted on" to the R/3 system. Network connectivity is established.

Finally, the system is tested in a production environment.

Much time and effort must be spent on executing the conversions and the interfaces. Data conversions are performed, monitored, and spot tested. Interfaces are ported to the production environment. Then, it is confirmed that they are operational.

Users must be trained using the materials created during the transition phase. Trainers must be trained first, so they can train all users without having to have the SAP implementation do all of the training.

Exhibit 18.3   Transition

Tasks	Key Deliverables	Tools & Techniques
• Confirm Readiness • Initiate Production	• Completed Transition Plan • Converted Data • Production SAP System • Mobilized Support Teams	• Readiness Checklist

Training material should use a number of media, written materials, interactive work on the system using training data rather than live data, and video. Training should be scheduled within six weeks of going live with the system. The training should be at the team's site, using the training system that has been created.

Exhibit 18.4   Go-Live Checklist

1. Has the system been tested and accepted by both users and the IT department?
2. Has the production environment been checked for readiness and tested?
3. Has the outstanding-issues list been cleared of critical items (show stoppers)?
4. Have all conversions been completed?
   Transaction data
   Master data
5. Have all interfaces been tested?
6. Have volume and stress tests been completed?
7. Has the back-up process been tested to ensure that a restore is possible?
8. Is a Fast Response Team in place to deal with production system problems?
9. Is a Help Desk in place and staffed?
10. Has disaster recovery and contingency planning been put in place?
11. Has user training been completed?
12. Do the users know the go-live status?
13. Has there been a readiness assessment?
14. Has final approval for go-live been given by the Steering Committee and Internal Audit?
15. Has a post-implementation review been scheduled?

Assessing readiness to move to a live production system means confirming the system availability, as well as the readiness of users and of data. When all three of these variables are ready to go live, one can cut over to an R/3 production environment and turn off legacy systems. See Exhibit 18.4 for a checklist for going live.

SUSTAIN

The final stage in the implementation life cycle is to sustain the system. The purpose of the sustain module is to ensure the consistent review of system and business process performance metrics and the identification of action plans to sustain competitive advantage. Exhibit 18.5 shows the tasks and key deliverables of this phase, as well as the tools and techniques used.

This stage of work covers updating documentation, reviewing the project work, and confirming that the system as it has been put in place meets business objectives.

All documentation, user training, and operations must be updated to reflect any changes that were made during the implementation.

The project team's work should be reviewed. Lessons learned from the efforts need to be consolidated for future efforts, as they pertain both to

Exhibit 18.5   Sustain

Tasks	Key Deliverables	Tools & Techniques
• Consolidate • Post Implementation Review • Track Performance Metrics	• Action Plans • Change Mgmt Program • Perf. Improv. Program • Post-implementation Review Report • Performance Metrics Matrix & Variance Analysis • Updated Performance Targets	• Change Management Techniques • Performance Measurement Analysis • Walkthroughs, Workshops & Questionnaires • RAISE

| Project Management |
| Change Management |
| Performance Measurement |

future SAP projects and to major change initiatives in general. Finally, these lessons must be communicated throughout the organization.

Performance has to be tracked against business goals, using appropriate metrics, and any follow-on actions need to be determined to make sure the system is able to provide the kind of business improvements for which it was implemented.

19

Deployment Options

After all of the back-end work has been done to install and implement SAP's R/3 software and prepare the organization to deploy the software within the business processes and systems, it is time to deploy the system.

It is important here to be clear about definitions. Installation is actually getting the software onto the hardware on which it will run. Implementation is configuring the various screens on the modules to present data in the proper form and collate that data into usable information. Both installation and implementation are back-office tasks; they are transparent to the front-end users and to customers.

Deployment is actually getting the system into the hands of the front-end users. A decision on which deployment option to use should come from executive management, not from the project management of the R/3 undertaking. The company's top managers must understand the implications of all the deployment options and make an informed choice as to which to use.

There are four options for the actual deployment.

1. **The Big Bang.** In the Big Bang approach, all modules are deployed in all processes at once. This can be at an entire company or at one division, business unit, or site. The Big Bang approach is the highest risk, but if it is done properly, it provides the fastest implementation. It is imperative

for companies trying this approach to train the entire organization ahead of the deployment.

2. **By R/3 Module.** Most companies that choose this option start by deploying the finance modules or the sales and distribution modules first, and letting that choice drive the rest of the deployment.

3. **By Business Process.** An example of this would be deploying all of the modules necessary to deal with requisition to payment. An example of this type of deployment is a major U.S. defense contractor that has three customers and deploys an entire SAP R/3 system at each customer site to support the particular processes the company and each customer have to requisition and pay for product.

4. **Pilot/Rollout.** This method can work in conjunction with either the first or the second method. A company can do a Big Bang at one site as a pilot, then repeat that effort at successive sites, learning from each deployment to make future deployments run more smoothly; or it can deploy one module at one site, then simultaneously roll out that module to other sites while deploying a second module at the initial site, and so on until all the modules are deployed in all of the sites where they are necessary.

Whatever option you pick, do not fall into the trap one U.S. high-tech company did of letting each business unit decide its own deployment strategy. The business units ended up competing with each other so much for which could deploy R/3 the fastest that none of the deployments were successful. This company forgot that R/3 is an enterprise solution. Each business unit was driven to a different deployment approach by a different set of goals and pressures. Each hired its own consultants. In sum, the situation was chaos.

FACTORS THAT AFFECT DEPLOYMENT AND THE APPROACH TAKEN

Which deployment approach you take will be affected by the time in which you have to work and the resources—people and dollars—you are willing to put into the effort. The size and scope of your effort will also affect the decision of which deployment approach to take. Finally, there are a number of major events that may be pushing you toward an SAP R/3 implementation that will also have an effect on which deployment approach you take. Among these are the following:

o Merger or divestiture
o Year 2000 problems in your current system
o Increasing software failures in your current system
o A current re-engineering effort within your company
o Austerity and cost-cutting programs within your company

Overlaying these issues that affect your decision are another set of issues that affect the deployment, whichever deployment approach you choose. To some degree, these issues will steer you toward one deployment approach over another, but they will have an impact no matter which deployment approach you decided on. Among them are the following:

o **Geography.** Is your company domestic, regional, or global; and do you want your deployment and implementation of R/3 to be domestic only, regional, or country-by-country?

o **Customer needs.** Are certain customers, or certain sets of customers, demanding information and information transfer that your current systems are not capable of performing?

o **User needs.** Which user in your company is driving the decision to obtain, install, and deploy R/3? Is it the financial community, or the information technology (IT) community? Is it the sale and marketing community who are reflecting customer needs?

o **Time and urgency.** If your current software systems are experiencing increased and increasingly costly failures, you need to get R/3 up and running somewhat quickly. If you are using SAP's software as a correction for Year 2000 problems rather than reworking your current software, you are also facing time pressures.

  ○ **Legacy system impact.** Different deployment options have a different impact on your current systems. A limited rollout for a division will probably mean that legacy systems used by other divisions will not be decommissioned and that maintenance costs will be ongoing.

KEYS TO DEPLOYMENT SUCCESS

As with any major organizational change effort, an SAP R/3 implementation and deployment needs full-time and focused commitment from management. Of course, executive managers cannot give the effort their full attention, but they must appoint one person high enough in the management organization to champion the effort, and that champion must keep the executive team well enough briefed that they can speak intelligently about the effort.

The deployment cannot run smoothly unless the scope of the system's use has been defined and finalized early in the project. If the scope is not understood and agreed to by all at the time of deployment, you run the risk of encountering scope creep, where the scope keeps growing as you deploy. This usually leads to chaos.

One company in the Southeast United States did not define its scope before it began deploying SAP. At the height of its effort, the company had 750 of its own people working on building the new system, but because there was no sense of scope, different business functions and different business units were working on the system in completely different ways. These 750 people were all in one building, but they weren't talking to one another.

The company finally called a halt to trying to build the system itself and called in a consulting firm that specializes in turnkey systems (doing it to you). The first thing the consulting firm did was sit down with the company's executive management team and begin defining the project's scope.

Along with defining and finalizing the scope, the deployment strategy must be defined and finalized before the actual deployment begins. The execution of the deployment effort can be distributed, but the creation of a deployment strategy needs to be centralized.

You must focus full-time in-house resources into the deployment. The people who work on the deployment should be some of the company's best, they cannot be people between assignments or those who you are looking to put on the shelf for a couple of years to allow them to accrue time toward a better pension. Their absence from the day-to-day operations of the ongoing business has to hurt the organization. Remember: No pain, no gain.

Change management practices begun early in the effort must continue through the deployment. People need to be constantly aware of the state of the effort. Communication must be constant and truthful.

End users must be trained ahead of the deployment, and their training needs to continue through the deployment. Trainers need to be trained so they can move the effort deeper into the organization. Training should begin at the end of scope definition. A training system should be constructed with sample data, so people get used to manipulating the kind of data they will actually be using, and turning that data into information. Training materials need to be created, including software, paper text, audio, and video.

Finally, and possibly most important, executive management must agree to the R/3 release it will use. Since a full R/3 installation and deployment takes from one to two years, and since SAP comes out with a new release every nine months to one year, you could be two and possibly even three releases behind by the time your system is fully operational. Top management must be able to live with this. It is impossible to jump from one release to the next in the middle of your effort, since you will have to go back and reconfigure all that has already been configured according to the previous release.

PROBLEMS COMMONLY FACED IN DEPLOYMENT

There are a number of problems common to most SAP R/3 undertakings.

A whole set of problems revolve around resources, especially people. One major problem is that companies that are behind yours in their SAP effort or are just now thinking about an enterprise solution may look to raid your company and take your best SAP practitioners from you. Some companies are finding it necessary to lock their best SAP minds in with "stay bonuses" on top of salary. Some of these bonuses are running to the high five or low six figures annually.

Also, when you move from deploying R/3 at one to many sites, the number of people you need in the effort expands exponentially rather than arithmetically. Some people will be busy working with users at the new site, and others will be busy coordinating the efforts of the many sites.

Training enough trainers to train everyone in the organization is another resource issue that often comes up. Not everyone has the ability to train others, so you cannot just have one person train 10, each of whom will then train 10 more. You need to find one good trainer for every 100 to 200 people to be trained.

Another problem common to many R/3 undertakings is dealing with constant software upgrades. One large oil company was going into the system test portion of deployment when SAP released version 5.0 of R/2 to replace version 4.3. The company decided to take the software upgrade and reopen its system design. This led to huge bottlenecks as tables had to be reconfigured and processes redesigned. As stated previously, every company has to put its stake in the sand at some point and say that it will not chase after increased functionality in the next R/3 release at the expense of redoing all the configuration work that has already been done. There may be a totally new module released that would be very useful to you, however, or a third-party provider may release a new tool that would be very useful.

Each of these instances will cause some reconfiguration. Each has to be weighed in terms of the extra effort necessary against the payoff from undertaking the extra effort.

Finally, among global companies, there is the issue of global implementation and deployment. A 24-hour help line should be established for any user around the world to contact. This is a huge resource to create and maintain.

IMPLICATIONS OF POOR DEPLOYMENT

Poor deployment has a number of outcomes, none of which are fun to deal with.

First, if executive management decides that the effort is worth it despite the poor deployment, massive rework will be involved in order to do it right. This may mean going back nearly to the beginning of the project and defining the scope, re-implementing and configuring, and retraining.

Another implication is simple nonacceptance of the system and the processes designed by users. If people refuse to use the system, it is not worth much. If a situation exists of nonacceptance by users and executives who insist on redoing the effort, there could ultimately be a cataclysmic crash.

While redoing the effort is one option, simply halting the project is the other. Many companies do not like to admit failure, so they term this a project put on indefinite hold.

Whether the project is halted or tried again, the bottom line is that expectations are not met. In the end, being in the top level of managing such a project with unmet expectations can lead to career opportunities being sidetracked or missed altogether. The bottom line for implementors and project managers is to force executive managers to define goals and objectives, accept the costs and risks inherent in the undertaking, and stick with the program through the natural problems that it will encounter.

DEPLOYMENT EXAMPLES: SUCCESSFUL AND UNSUCCESSFUL

Personal Computer Company—Successful

This large manufacturer of personal computer (PC) products took the Big Bang approach, first in Europe with the financial accounting (FI), controlling (CO), materials management (MM), sales and distribution (SD), and production planning (PP) modules. Key issues the company addressed were European statutory requirements. The design took eight months to complete, followed by a five-month rollout at 22 sales locations and one factory in Europe. One of the major problems the company faced was the time required to test and the completeness of the testing.

Utility Company—Successful

This company did a domestic Big Bang of the FI, CO, MM, and project system (PS) modules for 3,500 users. This implementation included support from multiple consulting firms, all of which were controlled effectively by the company's program management group. This implementation was completed in 21 months over 100 sites in one state in the United States.

Auto Manufacturer—Successful

This company took a combined Big Bang and modular approach. An integrated solution, other than a common chart of accounts, was not an objective. This project had strong management commitment, combined with an ability to make timely decisions throughout the project. Additionally, scope creep was aggressively controlled.

Major Manufacturer—Semi-Successful

This company wanted an enterprise-wide solution across the domestic U.S. business. The company separated the implementation teams by process (SD, finance, procurement/accounts payable (AP), and manufacturing). The company did not finalize/understand the SAP hierarchy implications and believed that it could fix differences later with little rework. The company ended up with four systems, and four different numbering schemes, for the same inventory. The system was not integratable; the company now estimates that rework will take approximately one year. The company is also now looking for Year 2000 alternatives.

Paper Manufacturer—Unsuccessful

This organization did not have senior management support. Program management did not exist, and the implementation teams were not coordinated. The project never met deadlines and soon was stopped by management and re-organized to include a large system integrator, who in effect is now completing the project.

National Postal Service—Thought to be a success, then realized to be unsuccessful

Financial modules were developed first without an understanding of the migration across SAP. This company inappropriately used the plant field for financial purposes, without understanding the impact on inventory in subsequent phases. When MM was implemented, it was apparent that the material master file would have to be duplicated at each site because of the misuse of the plant field. The system is currently being re-implemented.

20

Integration Management

Most purchases of SAP R/3 software are made because of the integration of function and information available throughout the system. However, integration occurs only if the SAP system is configured to be integrative. It does not happen by default; it must be a conscious effort.

Because it is possible to implement SAP as individual functional modules, if the task of integration management is not taken on during the implementation, there will be no integration when the system becomes live. Unless integration is closely managed, the implementation will disintegrate into chaotic chunks of functionality.

Integration management is too big a task to be undertaken by a single individual. Rather, it is the purview of a small team, usually two to four members. Within this team, there must be individuals with different focuses of knowledge. There must be at least one individual with a close working knowledge of the business's processes. This person must be open minded about redesigning those processes. There must be a person with a close working knowledge of the company's legacy systems, yet open minded about replacing those systems with appropriate SAP modules. There must also be a person with detailed knowledge of critical SAP modules and the enterprise module.

The role of the integration management team should not be confused with the role of project or program management. The integration team will work at the nitty-gritty level of detail. While the team must be made up of individuals who are good communicators and diplomats, they must also be willing to ram through necessary steps in the process if necessary.

They must find the areas between implementation teams in which there is likely to be some conflict in the future, and work to defuse the conflict before it even begins.

A number of other benefits accrue from a close management of system integration. The business receives the following:

- Cooperating systems and benefits
- Maximum benefit from the installation of an SAP system
- The ability to determine throughout the implementation process exactly which parts of the SAP software are applied appropriately
- The ability to identify issues earlier and possibly avoid having to redo work
- Better communication between teams around key integration points
- Establishment of data standards, codes, and usage as the effort moves along

Integration management is an ongoing task that stops after a postimplementation review. The job is focused on getting SAP to meet the company's business objectives and assuring that a realistic SAP design is put into place that works with the company's other information technology (IT) systems. It involves making sure that data is defined to meet business needs, that business processes within SAP talk to each other, and that SAP systems are all in communication with each other and with legacy systems, as well as managing the scope of the SAP system.

It is important for the person who fulfills this role to have a firm understanding of how SAP is applied, where it should be applied, and where it should not.

Integration management is not process design, system design, project management, change control, or the basis system. All of these other areas are separate and distinct from integration management.

SAP SYSTEM ARCHITECT

The SAP system architect is the person with a deep knowledge of the SAP system who leads the small team responsible for overall integration for SAP itself and for SAP in the total systems environment. The person who fills this role must be an excellent communicator and facilitator, as well as a lateral thinker, who thinks in terms of processes rather than functions. The system architect must be conversant with SAP, at least to the degree of understanding the financial accounting (FI), controlling (CO), sales and distribution (SD), materials management (MM), and production planning (PP) modules and submodules for a manufacturing implementation.

The system architect should have prior experience with an SAP implementation and a firm understanding of the SAP enterprise model. This person should be a realist, understanding not only what SAP can do but, more importantly, what it cannot do.

It is unlikely you will be able to locate, recruit, and hire such an individual. They are coveted by their present employers, and often paid enormous sums. This is one of the areas in which it is nearly imperative that you turn to an SAP consultancy for help.

TASKS OF INTEGRATION MANAGEMENT DURING THE PHASES OF THE IMPLEMENTATION LIFE CYCLE

In this chapter, as in Chapters 17 and 18, we are again looking at the life cycle of an implementation effort through the lens of our particular methodology, Summit R/3. Whatever the terminology is in the particular methodology you use, all of the tasks must be undertaken, grouped as they are here.

Initiation

During this phase, the task of the integration team is to identify the main SAP modules that are needed to meet the business's needs, and to note the major gaps between the legacy systems and the SAP system. Information Technology strategy should be fed into the integration team at this point, so it knows which legacy systems will stay up and which are to be decommissioned.

Strategy Analysis

During this phase, the tasks include mapping SAP functions to the key requirements, identifying advanced business application programming (ABAP) or customization needs, validating the system topology, and continuing to identify gaps. Here, the team starts to look at the structure of the business and at the SAP enterprise model and tries to match them. Work begins here with key, high-level system users.

Process Design

During this phase, the task is to validate that SAP is able to support designed processes and to note where the software cannot support design processes. Here, the committee begins to look at bolt-on software that can be used to fill in gaps between legacy systems and SAP, and gaps in what the business needs to do and where SAP is not strong.

The integration team also looks closely at touch points where business processes touch. Members begin seeing who expects to be a feeder from their process into another process and who expects to be fed. Paper route maps are drawn, then workshops are held with the implementation teams about handoffs and touch points, so that when they really occur no one will drop the ball.

Also, at this point, the integration team begins organizing site visits for implementation teams. Executives have already made site visits as part of their education process prior to purchasing the system and engaging in the effort, but now the folks actually carrying out the implementation begin to visit companies that have done it successfully before.

The role of integration management in these first three phases is seen in Exhibit 20.1.

Prototype/Develop

In this phase, there are six major tasks.

1. Ensure that a fully integrated system is designed and configured, focusing on configuration, master data, data standards, definitions and usage, and interfaces and conversions. At this point, everyone needs to be speaking the same language.

2. Facilitate identification and resolution/escalation of major issues to the program manager for resolution. The integration team needs to bring together these relevant parties.

3. Coordinate integration meetings, find the touchpoints that might have been missed previously, and work to resolve any potential to miss handoffs.

4. Documentation. This involves establishing integration test scenarios, designing user training, and creating operations procedures.

5. Look carefully at how interfaces will work. This involves going to the business units and seeing that customizations or upgrades of legacy systems are properly coordinated.

6. Integration team needs to plan an end-to-end test of the system.

Exhibit 20.1 Integration Management in the Life Cycle Modules Initiation, Strategy Analysis, Process Design

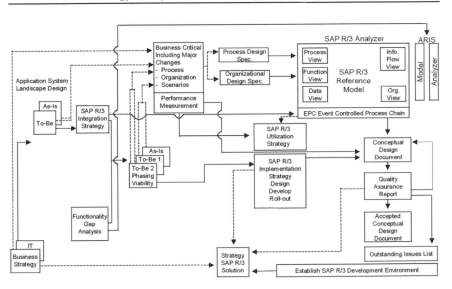

Exhibit 20.2   Integration Management in the Life Cycle Modules Prototype
and Develop

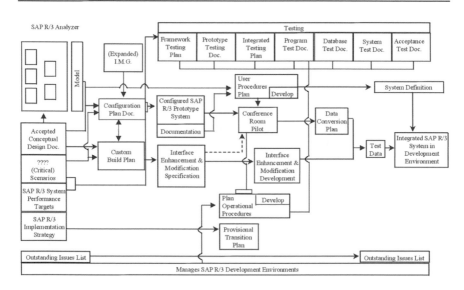

The role of integration management in these next two phases are shown in Exhibit 20.2.

Transition

In this phase, the implementation team oversees testing and validates results. The team also begins work on sustaining the system, ensuring that the system meets expectations for performance and integration, and creating a mechanism for ongoing production support.

At this point, the implementation team also needs to make sure that knowledge has been properly transferred to those who will support the installed system. The team may need to do some formal design work of the support team.

The role of integration management in these last two phases of the implementation life cycle are shown in Exhibit 20.3.

In some implementations, the integration team is brought back together after the system is up and running for three to six months to examine how to achieve all the benefits that the company had hoped to achieve.

Exhibit 20.3   Integration Management in the Life Cycle Modules Transition
& Sustain

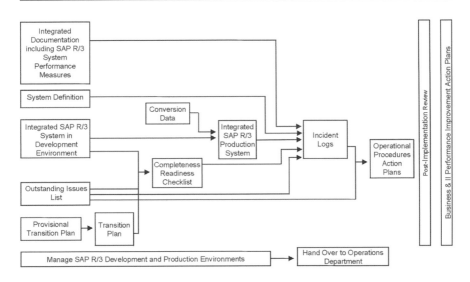

This might involve putting in some continuous improvement plans or tin-
kering with some of the handoffs between modules. Other companies have
an independent reviewer come in from outside to do this review.

Whichever way the review is conducted, it is important that the integration team be involved in any changes made to the system. If no one
who has an overview of the system is allowed to make even tiny changes,
the system could be greatly damaged. The integration team must sign off
on any changes made after the installation is complete.

INTEGRATION MANAGEMENT IS KEY

Integration management is one of the most important roles in the entire
SAP implementation. To ignore it is to put the implementation in peril.
The integration team is the place to put the company's best and brightest.
It is the place for which to recruit personnel. It is the place to spend extra
to bring in the best consulting system architect possible.

Integration management ties back to the real reason your company
bought the SAP software. Much of the cost of implementing SAP R/3 has
real worth only if you achieve the benefits of system integration.

21

SAP Tools

Along with the body of its enterprise resource software, SAP has created a set of tools for implementation of the software configurations and development of customized environments, using SAP's programming language, ABAP4. These tools can be very helpful during the implementation effort, as can some other tools that have been developed by other companies with SAP's blessing. (These other tools are the subject of Chapter 20.)

The Accelerated SAP (ASAP), methodology was discussed in Chapter 10. This chapter will concentrate on the Business Engineering Workbench (BEW), which is the basic set of tools available in R/3, and give some information on the new Business Engineer that is part of Release 4.0 and in many ways supersedes many of the BEW functions.

BUSINESS ENGINEERING WORKBENCH

The business engineering workbench is the name given to the collection of tools used for configuring the R/3 software. The following are the main components of the BEW:

- R/3 procedure model
- R/3 reference model/process model
- Implementation guide (IMG)

R/3 Procedure Model

This is SAP's procedures for implementing the system. It is a general overview, at a higher level than the typical methodology. The procedure model had passed for a time as SAP's methodology, but customers found it quite lacking, since it defines procedures at such a general level. The ASAP methodology essentially supersedes this.

However, the procedure model is complementary with other methodologies such as ASAP and Coopers & Lybrand's Summit R/3. In this way, it can be used as a pocket guide of sorts, or a "crib sheet." However, it says nothing about change management or knowledge transfer, and little about process redesign or re-engineering.

The procedure model covers the life cycle of an implementation in the following four phases:

1. Organization and conceptual design
2. Detailed design and implementation
3. Preparation for production
4. Productive operation

The procedure model also covers system maintenance and release upgrades.

Reference Model/Process Model

The reference model illustrates the functionality and business processes provided with SAP. There are five main views.

1. Process view
2. Data view
3. Distribution model
4. Business object model (e.g., customers, cost centers, etc.)
5. Organization view

The most commonly used view is the process model, or event process chain, as shown in Exhibit 11.2. This shows a series of business events by process steps. Each process step maps to an SAP translator. The model shows the details of using SAP to complete the process.

These views are used by the third-party process-modeling tools that are partners with SAP; these became available with Release 2.1. They allow the models to be mobilized to reflect customizations made to the system.

From Release 3.0, SAP provides the Business Navigator, which allows users to view the processes on line as part of R/3, but not to modify them. The Business Navigator does, however, allow users to drill down on individual process steps to see the SAP transactions used to process them. From here, it is possible to link to the IMG and tables used to configure that specific process step.

Implementation Guide

The IMG is an on-line configuration tool that lists tables and activities required to configure the system. It is a tool for documenting and controlling the configuration. It works module by module, beginning with global settings (e.g., country) and the enterprise structure. From there, you work your way down deeper and deeper into the system's modules.

SAP'S DEMO MODEL

The International Demonstration and Education System (IDES) was shipped as part of R/3. It is a preconfigured model of an international company (either European-based or U.S.-based). The company operates in a number of different accounting and manufacturing environments.

SAP argues that the IDES provides speed in training, in developing a pilot, and in decision making, and competence and effectiveness in daily business tasks.

The IDES provides a training ground for project teams and a base for configuration development in small to medium-sized companies. It is less useful for large companies.

The IDES really is nothing more than a good "sandbox" tool, a place to try out different things in an SAP environment without having to build your own demo platform.

BUSINESS ENGINEER

Business Engineer is available beginning with Release 4.0. It is a configuration and implementation tool that includes the reference model and replaces most of the engineering workbench.

Business Engineer uses a question-and-answer approach to configuring the enterprise model. It uses business scenarios, organizations, processes, and functions, and simplifies the configuration compared to earlier SAP configuration tools.

Most important, the question-and-answer format allows Business Engineer to validate the configuration. If a query is answered in a way that is inconsistent with previous answers, the configuration becomes invalid, and the program goes back to the place in the series of queries where the configuration went wrong.

As the configuration proceeds in a valid way, the tool documents the configuration.

In addition to the "configurator" and the reference model, Business Engineer also has an R/3 repository that stores reference models, enterprise models, and industry-specific models. A repository interface allows non-SAP tools to access the repository. This flexibility allows a host of third-party tools to be used as adjuncts to the SAP tools during the implementation.

22

Third-Party Tools

As previously stated, SAP has reviewed and approved literally dozens of third-party providers to sell software tools that can be used to enhance both the implementation of an R/3 system and the operations of that system. This chapter describes some of those types of tools.

It must be noted that the list of tools is growing literally by the week. Between the time this book was written and the time you read it, there will undoubtedly be new and in many cases better tools on the market. Our recommendations are based on personal use of tools. Because of this, the discussion is of necessity more useful on a generic level and should not be read as "product reviews."

There are four types of tools. See also Exhibit 22.1.

1. Implementation tools
2. Archiving and warehousing tools
3. System and network management tools
4. Communication tools.

Exhibit 22.1   Third-Party Tools

Types of Tools

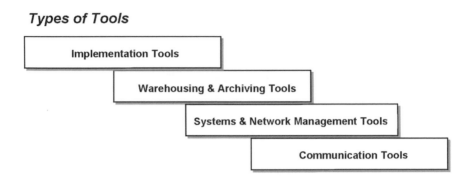

IMPLEMENTATION TOOLS

Process Modeling Tools

Process modeling tools provide the ability to model a business and its processes, and link those processes directly to SAP functions. The best process modelers take one right to the appropriate SAP screen.

Modeling software allows you to walk through process variants and choose the best, then link the process path you have chosen to the particular screens for SAP. They allow you to understand how SAP will work in the business environment, as well as showing you how SAP will run optimally. They allow you to see how you can change the way you run your business.

These software packages allow you to capture and track changes to the process design as you go and to document your decisions for SAP configuration in a common repository.

Benefits of Using Process Modeling Tools.   If this technology is used correctly, you can gain many benefits in your implementation. With Release 4.0, SAP is moving closer to having an ability to track process design decisions and to having a common repository for different teams to put their decisions into. Process modeling software is good for team communications, allowing teams to put their work in a common repository, enhancing integration of effort.

Modeling software allows you to establish a business blueprint quickly and effectively, and to respond to changes to that blueprint in real time. You can validate decisions early, prior to going live.

This enhanced communication and ability to look at your process design in real time is extremely helpful in controlling scope. You can see through the modeling software exactly what ripple effects will occur as you change one process, and can decide where to draw the boundaries of your implementation.

Characteristics of the Best. The best process modelers have the following characteristics:

o They link to the SAP implementation guide (IMG).
o They are easy to use.
o They work across and integrate process design for multiple Enterprise Resource Planning (ERP) solutions. In other words, you can model processes and show how these processes will interact not only with SAP R/3 software, but also with Baan and PeopleSoft software.
o They help in moving toward an automated configuration.
o They are compliant with the unified modeling language (UML).
o They link to the Internet.

Some Titles. To our way of thinking, the most advanced of these tools is Livemodel, by Intellicorp. In fact, SAP has started to incorporate parts of this software into its basic package, beginning with Release 4.0. We use it in our implementation consulting work. Other programs are IDS Scheer's ARIS and Visio Corporation's Visio.

Documentation Tools

Documentation tools are used both during implementation and during the production phase of R/3. We have listed them in the implementation tools because, when used correctly, they are initially used in implementation to help create both system and user documentation.

These tools facilitate creation of documentation. They provide control and security documentation, as well as creation and maintenance documentation. They can create hyperlinks and thereby provide diagnostic and help documents.

The best provide both the ability to migrate (to upgrade as SAP software achieves more functionality) and to integrate SAP software with desktop software for "helps" and for training. With them—the most prominent being Microscoft's Office 97—you can access help documentation from within SAP.

Benefits of Using Documentation Tools.   If this technology is used correctly, consistency in system and user documentation is ensured, the production of documentation is accelerated, and at the end of the day there is a central and controllable repository of both system and user documentation.

Some Titles.   The best example of a documentation tool is Insite Objects Inc.'s Docsite. Other providers are Documentation Associates and information Mapping (IMAP). SAP's ASAP methodology will soon provide a tool to assist with documentation.

ARCHIVING AND WAREHOUSING TOOLS

Data Archiving Tools

Archiving tools provide backup and recovery capabilities for SAP R/3 systems. Remember, once an SAP system is up and running, there will be literally terabytes of data on the system. This type of software manages the backing up without human intervention.

These tools provide for unattended operation and work through a centrally controlled, integrated facility. They provide multiple and simultaneous backup of many databases to many storage systems. They perform dynamic routing based on storage system availability and restart options in case of failure during operation.

These tools support many storage devices and databases, such as Oracle, Informix, and Sybase. They provide security to allow or stop access, and can enable or disable devices.

They manage and inventory tapes, cleaning them and ultimately disposing of them. They provide off-site storage and management of tape libraries and perform search and retrievals based on multiple criteria.

Benefits of Using Data Archiving Tools. If this technology is used the right way, you take the load off your system, not allowing it to get too full. They save time and space by compressing data and providing access to old documents. They provide security and save system resources by allowing you to load and repeat processing or reports without having to recrunch the numbers.

Some Titles. Examples include the following:

o SCH: dbBRZ for R/3, REELbackup
o Alexandria: Backup and Archive Librarian
o Amdahl: A+ Software
o Seagate Software: Backup Exec
o Computer Associates: Unicenter TNG

Data and Report Warehousing

This is the type of software that allows data to be collated from both your SAP system(s) and other systems and fed back through SAP and your executive information system (EIS). This type of software can be used to design, build, and manage data warehouses, as well as to store, extract, and report data from different data sources.

These programs allow a number of different types of queries to be performed—simple queries, comparative queries, and forecasting and what-if analytical queries. Data can be compiled and reported in text, graphics, pictures, or tables.

Warehousing tools are often seen as panaceas to companies with multiple systems and varied data. They are not. Careful system design always delivers the best information. In the past, SAP's report-writing capabilities have been limited, although the company is bringing out its own data warehouse.

Benefits of Using Data and Report Warehousing Tools.   If this technology is used to its fullest, you get all the data necessary to create the right information and the right level of specificity for the audience, at the time you need it. You get fast and easy access, with data that is consistent across the enterprise.

Report writing is made faster, with reduced effort to print and distribute reports, and reduced costs of information access.

Characteristics of the Best.   The best data and report warehousing software provides open interfaces with all database software and packages, as well as the ability to store reports locally or system-wide. They allow you to integrate information from Web sites into your reports, and even use Web servers as storage sources and as destinations (i.e., you can distribute your report via the Web.)

Some Titles.   Examples of warehousing software are Arcplan's InSight, Quest Software's Vista Plus, Software AG's SourcePoint, Oracle's Express, and Brio's Enterprise.

SYSTEM AND NETWORK MANAGEMENT TOOLS

This type of software provides distributed network applications systems management across the enterprise. It monitors multiple R/3 systems and other applications over multiple platforms and measures deployment, performance, and operations. It inventories information technology (IT) assets and provides security for multiple sites.

Network management tools can be used to identify which version of software is being used and automatically distribute updates to that version, as well as monitoring the system at the event level, transaction by transaction.

The software allows you to monitor communications responses, which systems are on- or off-line, as well as server, database, and operating system performance. It can perform predictive analysis and automated diagnosis of service levels, and centrally administer and monitor workloads for multiple R/3 systems.

Benefits of Using System and Network Management Tools.   If these tools are used correctly, your computer center management system capabilities are extended across platforms and systems, and the reliability and manage-ability of the IT environment in general is improved. System availability, service levels, and integrity in general are improved, and, most of all, downtime is reduced.

Perhaps the greatest benefit of this type of software is that it allows the IT organization to manage a rapidly growing computing infrastructure without increasing the staff. Some companies have doubled the size of their IT infrastructure every year. This software allows each individual to significantly increase productivity in hardware management.

Some Titles.   Examples of system and network management tools are Tivoli's YME 10, Computer Associates' Unicenter TNG, Envive's Inspector, Amdahl's A+ software, and a number of products from Seagate.

SAP Change Control Software

Although change control software focuses on user functionality rather than system maintenance per se, it is included in this section.

This type of software allows one to document change requests cen-trally and define ownership and status of objects, or named items, in the SAP hierarchy. There are interfaces with the IMG and the correction and transfer (CTS) modules in SAP.

Using this software allows one to know which configuration of which version of R/3 is on which box within the system. These programs provide good audit trails of changes made.

Titles.   Insite Objective Inc.'s product, Insite, is a good example.

COMMUNICATION TOOLS

Electronic Data Interfacing

This type of software provides a means of exchanging data between differ-ent systems in both standard and custom formats.

These tools provide for different electronic data interchange (EDI) standards and integrate with SAP software and data structures. In other words, they can speak in many different languages. They provide automatic EDI within a business process and build interfaces between systems as needed.

This type of software can be used to integrate with trading partners for easier and quicker transfer of purchase and sale information with no custom coding. This provides lower maintenance and greater reliability.

Some Titles. We particularly like two products in this area: Harbinger's Trusted Link and TSI's Mercator. Other products are Envisionit's Visualflow and various products by Premenos.

World Wide Web Technology

Technology is rapidly coming on-line to extend the World Wide Web into an organization's SAP application, providing a Web front end for SAP applications for existing functionality, as well as for bringing together multiple data sources for SAP from Web-native applications. In other words, any SAP application can now be made to look like a Web page. (SAP is also developing rapidly in this area, and Release 4.0 will have a JAVA engine.)

This technology has the potential to make communications more effective, integrating customers, suppliers, employees, and business units, and to make payments and collections more seamless by utilizing Web applications such as information about U.S. sales and use taxes. It can also reduce the need for training by utilizing familiar web browsers.

At its highest potential use, it can streamline information transfer and improve global business processes, allowing the enterprise to deliver products and services globally and efficiently.

Some Titles. Two titles come to mind: NetDynamics' WebEXTEND and products from Pandesic.

Fax and Telephony Tools

These tools provide integration of phone, voice, fax, e-mail, pagers, and the World Wide Web for SAP functions in a heterogeneous environment.

They integrate with SAPconnect and SAPcomm communications servers to make faxes and standard output destination of all SAP applications. They provide central administration of fax and telephone functions over multiple SAP systems and automatically route incoming messages.

They can manage calls, forwarding, tracking, replying, scheduling calls, and managing a phone book.

These tools allow one to respond to customer queries quickly by allowing queries to the SAP systems using touch-tone phones to get order status and other information.

Some Titles. A few of the programs that perform these functions are SCH Technologies' Merkur, Edify's Electronic Workforce, and AMC's TDIS.

Imaging

Imaging is not a communication tool per se, but it does allow for enhanced communication, as well as enhanced reporting.

Imaging software allows images to be captured and attached to SAP transactions. Scanned documents, reports, and raw data can be stored and retrieved under the control of R/3 processes. A print list and reports that are stored on optical storage devices can also be retrieved.

They provide access across the Internet for administration, as well as the ability to manage scanners. Quality control editing can be performed, and there is security against unauthorized alterations.

Benefits of Using Imaging Software. Putting imaging software to its best use will allow customer service to be improved by providing access to original documents and conserving system resources with optical storage. Security, auditability, and control increase because paper is not used, thus eliminating the possibility of loss or alteration of paper reports and other data.

Some Titles. A couple of titles in the imaging area are iXos Software's Archive and Microsoft's FileNet.

SCAN THE MARKETPLACE

This is a rapidly changing area. New companies enter the fray every day, and current companies put out new products. SAP itself, which spends about $1 million a day every day of the year on research and development, is introducing new capabilities all the time. This chapter is only an introduction to some current tools. To be completely comprehensive would take a book in and of itself.

Before deciding on any tools, scan the marketplace, as well as the World Wide Web, then talk to SAP to see what is available at the time you are making your decision.

Glossary

ABAP/4 Fourth-generation programming language, developed by SAP, in which R/3 applications are written. ABAP stands for Advanced Business Application Programming.

ABAP/4 Data Dictionary Dictionary containing definitions of SAP technical objects, including data elements and tables.

ABAP/4 Workbench Development environment that contains tools for creating and maintaining business applications within the R/3 system. This includes a code editor, debugging tool, and screen painter.

ABC Analysis Analysis function within SAP reporting that allows the user to define criteria for grouping data in the report into three categories. Not to be confused with activity based costing.

ABC (Activity-Based Costing) An accounting method that accumulates all the costs in an organization related to a particular activity and determines a per unit cost for the activity to be carried out. These activity costs can be related to person power. For example, $25 per hour to provide the activity of typist which could include all costs related to this activity including salary, benefits, office space, cafeteria usage, and so on. Activity costs can also be related to machines. For example, $3 per mile to provide a delivery truck which could include depreciation, maintenance, gas, oil, licensing, and so on.

Activity (Network)	An activity is an instruction to perform a task within a network in a set period of time. Work, general costs, or external processing can be associated with it.
Activity-Based Costing	See *ABC*.
Activity Logs	Audit trail recording activity in the SAP R/3 system by user and transaction.
Activity Type	SAP master data element defining a service that can be provided by a cost center in discreet, measurable units. A cost is associated with each unit by cost center.
Actual Costs	Costs posted against a cost object. This includes both internal and external costs which are posted at the point of receipt by the cost object.
Advanced Business Application Program	See *ABAP/4*.
ALE Application Link Enabling	SAP method for passing documents between parts of an SAP system distributed across multiple instances.
AM	Asset management module, providing functionality for the financial management of fixed assets.
ASAP	Accelerated SAP. Rapid implementation methodology developed by SAP to reduce implementation timescales.
Asset Master	Master data record for financial fixed assets controlling the book and tax life and accounting for the asset.
AUC	Asset Under Construction. An asset record used to collect the costs of assets under construction prior to capitalization.
BASIS	SAP module providing technical functionality to develop and support a live SAP system. Functions include: system monitoring, security and authorizations, and custom code development.
Bill of Material	See *BOM*.
BIW	(Business Information Warehouse) SAP module, available from release 4.0, that provides data warehousing functionality.
BOM	(Bill of Material) List of component parts (materials or other BOMs) making a subassembly or assembly.

Budget	Funds authorized for spending against a project or project subdivision. The ability to post transactions to the project once these funds have been exceeded may be automatically controlled.
Business Area	Code used in the FI module to provide income statement and limited balance sheet reporting for divisions of a business, within or across legal entities.
Business Engineer	Question and answer based configuration tool available with R/3 from release 4.0.
Business Engineering Workbench	Tools supplied with standard SAP to assist in the design and configuration of the system.
Business Information Warehouse	See *BIW*.
Business Transaction	An SAP event creating a document that records a business event within the system.
Capacity	Resource available from a work center to perform a specific task.
Capacity Planning	Functionality provided by SAP to match available resources with demand for resource usage.
Classification System	SAP function available throughout the system to add user-defined criteria to SAP master data records. These criteria may then be used for reporting.
Client	A logical SAP system defined within an instance. Multiple clients share some common reference data (e.g., units of measure), but have distinct business processes, master data, and transaction data. Client is often used to define different environments during the development stage of a project, for example: prototyping, test, and live.
CO	Controlling module, providing management accounting functionality for internal reporting.
Company Code	Entity within a client that maintains a balancing set of books is used to define statutory reporting reports and processes.
Configuration	Development activity of making selections in SAP tables to define the way the system processes business events.

Controlling Area SAP entity within which management accounting and reporting take place. A controlling area may include one or more company codes for intercompany cost accounting.

Controlling Module See *CO*.

Cost Center Place in which costs are incurred for reporting or allocation to other organizational elements.

Cost Element Account for classifying costs for management accounting purposes. Cost elements are classified as primary for costs entering the business from outside sources, and secondary for cost movements with an internal impact only.

Cost Object SAP entity against which costs can be collected and reported for management purposes. Examples of cost objects include: cost centers, internal orders, work breakdown structure elements, network orders, maintenance orders, and service orders.

Cost Plan Plan of costs to be incurred against individual cost objects. Multiple plans may be created and reported against for each cost object.

Costing Calculated total production costs of individual goods or services.

Customer The customer record in SAP holds financial and logistical data required for taking orders, selling and shipping products and services, and collecting payment from customers.

Customizing Process of tailoring SAP software to meet the needs of a particular business.

Document SAP entity recording a particular business event, for example, invoice, journal entry, or material movement.

EC (Enterprise Controlling) SAP module providing enterprise wide data gathering and reporting. Functionality includes the Executive Information System and Profit Center Accounting.

Enterprise Model Set of interrelated business entities used to represent the enduring dimensions of a business, for example, legal entities and factories. These entities are created and maintained as part of the configuration of the system.

EPC (Event Driven Process Chain) SAP term for a process flow model representing business processes using a series of process steps and the events linking them.

ERP	(Enterprise Resource Planning) Term used to describe integrated software packages that can be used to plan and control resources across an entire business.
Event Driven Process Chain	See *EPC*.
FI	(Financial Accounting) SAP module providing functionality for statutory and external accounting reporting. The FI module also includes the accounts payable, accounts receivable, and special ledger functions.
Financial Accounting	See *FI*.
Graphical User Interface	See *GUI*.
Group Currency	Currency used by a group of companies to produce consolidated accounts.
GUI	(Graphical User Interface) The SAP GUI is designed to give the user a windows-based method of interacting with the system.
Hypertext	Online documentation that is set up in a network with active references pointing to additional text and graphics.
IDOC	(Intermediate document) An IDOC is a standard file layout used for passing data to and from an SAP system. The SAP R/3 system EDI (electronic data interchange) interface and the ALE program link enabling both use standardized intermediate documents to communicate.
Industry Solutions	See *IS*.
Instance	Physical installation of SAP software on a hardware platform, with a single physical database. Instances may be linked to form one logical system using ALE, or subdivided into functionally distinct systems, using client.
IMG	(Implementation Guide) An SAP provided tool that provides a detailed guide to the tables and steps required to configure the software. The IMG also provides tools for documenting and reporting against the progress of the configuration.
Intermediate Document	See *IDOC*.

Implementation Guide	See *IMG*.
IS	(Industry Solutions) SAP provided software modules that provide functionality to support the business requirements of specific industries or sectors. These are not provided as part of the standard software but must be purchased on an individual basis.
Local Currency	Currency in which the accounts of a company are held.
Master Data	Data representing individual business entities and which are used to process, classify, and report transactions within the system. These records are created and maintained by end users in the live system on a day-to-day basis.
Matchcode	Search tool provided by SAP to enable users to find master data and documents within the system. Matchcodes allow the user to enter data values and wild card characters for one or more data fields held on a record and retrieve a pick list of all records matching the criteria.
MM	Materials Management module. Module providing functionality for purchasing inbound logistics and material storage and movements within an organization. The materials management module includes MRP functionality.
Maintenance Order	Order type used to plan and execute maintenance on plant and equipment, collecting costs and a maintenance history.
Material	Master record used to describe goods and services that are purchased, created, modified, or sold by the business.
MRP	Materials Requirement Planning. System for automating materials replenishment to ensure continued production and supply while minimizing the level of stock held.
Network	Cost object allowing a user to define a series of tasks with the resources and time necessary to complete them. These tasks are linked by relationships that allow the system to calculate durations, float times, and critical paths for the completion of the network.
Operating Concern	An organizational unit to which one or more controlling areas can be assigned. The operating concern is used by the profitability analysis tool to combine cost and revenue data for internal management reporting.

Order Generic name for different cost objects used to gather costs and perform specific functions. Orders include: internal orders, network orders, maintenance orders, production orders, and service orders. Orders do *not* include purchase orders or sales orders.

Order/Project Results Analysis Periodic valuation of long-term orders and projects. The results analysis evaluates the costs and a measure of an order's progress toward completion, such as revenue booked or the quantity produced. Results analysis uses this information to calculate financial measures for the order/project including: cost of sales, capitalized costs or work in progress, capitalized profits, reserves for unrealized costs, reserves for the cost of complaints and commissions, and reserves for imminent loss.

Plan Version SAP allows the definition of up to 999 cost plans for cost objects, with each plan identified as a plan version. The number of plan versions available to end users is determined during configuration.

Plant Maintenance See *PM.*

PM (Plant Maintenance) SAP modules providing functionality to manage plant and equipment maintenance, planned and remedial. This module can be linked to the Asset Management (AM) module to provide integrated physical and financial management of assets.

PP Production Planning. SAP module used for planning and control of the manufacturing processes.

Primary Cost Planning Planning by values as well as quantities.

Primary Costs Costs incurred as a result of the consumption of goods and services from outside the business. For example, bought-in parts, raw materials, supplies, and services.

Production Costing SAP functionality provided by the PP and CO modules to calculate the costs of goods produced using a variety of cost accounting methods.

Production Order Order used to plan and execute the production of goods and services by manufacturing facilities.

Profit Center Master data item used by the Controlling and Enterprise Controlling modules of SAP. Profit centers gather costs posted against cost objects and revenues posted in the SD system to provide profit analysis for subdivisions of an organization. Profit centers can be linked into hierarchies and also provide some limited balance sheet performance indicators. It is possible to consolidate profit centers in the SAP consolidation module from release 4.0.

Profitability Analysis   Reporting tool provided as part of the controlling (CO) module to combine cost information with revenue from the sales and distribution module for profitability reporting. Analysis can be by account or a series of user defined reporting dimensions.

Project Definition   Framework laid down for all the objects created within a project. The data, such as dates and organizational data, are binding for the entire project.

PS   Project System. SAP module providing project management and accounting functionality.

Purchase Order   SAP document to purchase goods or services from an external vendor.

QM   Quality Management. SAP module providing functionality for managing quality in purchased and produced goods.

Relationship (Project System)   Link between two activities in a network order or across network orders. Four types of relationships are:

SS	start-start
FF	finish-finish
SF	start-finish
FS	finish-start

Results Analysis   SAP function to calculate the expected total costs, inventory, and reserves from planned costs, cost estimates, and level of completion for long-term orders and projects. The data calculated during results analysis is stored in the form of: cost of sales, capitalized costs, capitalized profit, reserves for unrealized costs, reserves for costs of complaints and commissions, and reserves for imminent loss.

Screen Painter   An SAP tool that can be used to create, modify, display, and delete screen diagrams.

SD
Sales and Distribution. SAP module providing functionality covering sales and outbound logistics from providing a customer with a quote to shipping and generating bills.

Secondary Cost Element
Cost centers require services from other cost centers to produce activity of their own. These are secondary costs. Planned assessment is used to plan the secondary cost quantities. Activity input is used to plan the secondary cost values.

Service Management Order
Order for managing work carried out on a customer's facilities as part of a warranty or service agreement.

Settlement
Process for clearing costs from orders and project work breakdown structure elements to other cost objects.

SM
Service Management. Module providing functionality to manage and perform work on a customer's installed base under warranty or service agreements.

Special Ledger
Part of the FI module providing additional financial ledgers for special processing requirements.

Transaction
Series of screens through which users process a business event to create either master data or a document.

Transaction Currency
Currency in which the actual business transaction was carried out.

Unit Costing
Method of costing where bills of material and routings are not used. Used to determine planned costs for assemblies or to support detailed planning of cost accounting objects, such as cost centers or orders.

User-Defined Fields
Entry fields that can be freely defined for an activity or a work breakdown structure element (project system) or an operation (production planning).

User Exit
Socket in a standard SAP transaction allowing a company to insert a custom developed process.

WBS
(Work Breakdown Structure) A model of a project. Represents in a hierarchy the actions and activities to be carried out on a project. Can be displayed according to phase, function, or object.

Work Breakdown Structure
See *WBS*.

Index

Index

Index